Faith Once Delivered

Sermons from Christ Church
by Paul N. Walker

A Mockingbird Publication
Charlottesville, VA

Mockingbird Ministries
100 W Jefferson St.
Charlottesville, VA 22902

FAITH ONCE DELIVERED
Sermons from Christ Church

Cover and book design by Ashley Rose Walton

ISBN - Hardcover: 978-1-7337166-2-8
ISBN - Paperback: 978-1-7337166-3-5

www.mbird.com

———

This collection of sermons
is dedicated with love and
gratitude to the people of Christ
Church, Charlottesville.

———

Contents

Preface

BY DAVID ZAHL

IT WAS A FEW MINUTES before noon on a Thursday, and I was killing time with Paul as he waited for his lunch date. We were standing at the bottom of the stairs at the office of Christ Church Charlottesville, as we often do. The young man arrived, and Paul introduced us. I had seen him at church but had yet to make his acquaintance.

After a few pleasantries, I asked how he had found our church. It's the sort of open-ended question that I had heard Paul ask newcomers before, the kind that allowed them to go as light or heavy as they wished. "Someone at the office invited me," one person might say, the next that her mother had recently died.

The young man responded by saying it was the sermons that had drawn him. He had never heard anything like them. He then paused, possibly debating whether or not to proceed with his next thought. After a moment he looked up at Paul and asked, "I've been listening for months and I have to ask: do you basically believe that people are always in a state of existential crisis?"

"Well, now that you mention it..." Paul responded, chuckling a little. "I suppose you could say that, yes."

The young man cracked his first smile, "So it's not just me!"

Their brief exchange crystallized something crucial for me about the nature of preaching, indeed the nature of life. I had only been working for Paul for a couple years at that point, but had been eagerly listening to his sermons for close to a decade. Some weeks I arrived at the sermon feeling fine, other weeks in a state of barely disguised distress. But no matter what attitude I brought to the pew or the iPod, I never walked away burdened. And I've never prepared a sermon myself without first consulting what Paul has said about the passage in question.

Some preachers conceive of their hearers as people who're doing basically okay but could use a pep talk. Some as pupils in need of instruction or wisdom. Some address the complacent person they feel needs to be jolted awake. But the audience Paul has in mind when he preaches are people undergoing some kind of crisis, existential or not. His words are aimed at the man or woman in pain. It turns out that describes all of us.

You might expect therefore that his sermons might be a little morose. Yet the exact opposite is true! Despite the gravity of what he has to say—indeed, because of it—there's a palpable freedom that comes across. Listen to him preach and you will hear a man who takes the Gospel seriously, but not himself. Or, put another way, a key part of Paul's task each time he climbs into the pulpit involves puncturing his audience's self-importance, beginning with his own. In poking fun at himself, he conveys that he is not above his hearers but right there among them, just as much in need of God's grace as anyone. It's a rare gift to be able to do so without attracting unnecessary attention, but Paul has it.

There are many other remarkable qualities I could commend in his sermons—the precision of the language, the literary imagination, the reverence of scripture, the sheer creativity. It's all there, in spades. But what most distinguishes the entries in this collection, what accounts for their urgency and power, is the message itself: the unflagging grace of God for non-theoretical sinners like you and me. This "goodest" of good news drips from every single sermon this man preaches.

Paul once told me that, since you never know who's sitting in the pew—perhaps they lost a loved one that week, or received a diagnosis, or simply got into a massive fight with their spouse on the way to church—you cannot risk preaching anything other than the forgiveness of sins. Any hedging and you'd be of more service selling insurance.

Of course, what we miss when the words are sequestered on the page is the sound of Paul's own voice. Because, as we all know, you can speak words of peace in an aggressive manner or words of absolution in a condemnatory tone. You can speak spiritual words without conviction or heart. As someone who was present for the majority of these sermons, you'll have to take my word for it when I say that the spirit in which they were delivered was one of utmost compassion, warmth, and sincerity.

And ultimately, that's why this man's ministry means so much to so many. Why his lunch schedule remains booked solid, year after year after year. These aren't just words. Paul is not merely a spokesman for God's grace but an active embodiment of it. He shows up on your worst day with arms outstretched and a listening ear (and possibly a well-mixed martini). That he would object to such a characterization, and resist any and all such lionization, only confirms its truth.

In fact, if you know Paul, then you know how grateful we should be that he agreed to let these sermons be preserved in the first place. Fortunately, this book was not his idea. Nor is the message it contains. It is nothing less than the faith once delivered and the only response to it is the only response to the preacher himself:

THANK YOU.

Now if you'll excuse me, I have an existential crisis that needs tending...

A Note on the Order of Things

WE'VE ORGANIZED THESE sermons by the liturgical calendar. That's an old way that Christians mark time, as a yearly pattern that follows events in the life of Jesus and the early church. It begins with Advent and continues into Christmas, Epiphany, Lent, Holy Week, Easter, and Pentecost.

Alongside this calendar, many churches follow a shared lectionary—a set of selections from Scripture that are assigned to be read each week. These readings rotate on a three-year cycle. Years A, B, and C center the Gospels of Matthew, Mark, and Luke, respectively. (Selections from John appear in each year.)

A few sermons in this collection don't follow the calendar or the lectionary. Some were delivered on a weekday, for Christ Church's college ministry or when the preacher was invited elsewhere. A few were preached after local tragedies. Brief notes in sermon headings provide any necessary explanation of circumstances.

November 28, 2010 ‡ *First Sunday of Advent (A)*

Cast Away the Works of Darkness

ISAIAH 2:1-5

William Golding's 1954 novel, *Lord of the Flies*, remains a piercing and, I believe, accurate judgment of human nature. In wartime, a group of English schoolboys are the only survivors of a plane crash on a paradisiacal yet deserted Island. They have no choice but to govern themselves.

It starts out well enough. The boys are happy to be free from adult restraint. They play on the beach and swim in the ocean. They elect leaders and formulate a plan for survival and rescue. One group of boys is in charge of hunting for food. Another group is in charge of keeping the rescue fire going.

Well, boys will be boys, right? Their attempt to govern themselves ends in disaster. They spend more time playing than working. The fire goes out. Factions arise. Fights break out. They resort to their most savage and violent instincts. Boys kill other boys.

The novel ends with the arrival of a British Naval Officer. When the remaining boys see him on the beach, they break down sobbing. They sob with relief at their rescue, and they sob in humiliation and sadness at what they have done to themselves and one another. The Naval Officer turns away, allowing the boys to get themselves together. He says he expected more from properly educated British boys.

I hope you will forgive me for beginning this sermon on such a dark note. I realize that, outside these church walls, Christmas has begun. After all, Santa himself was at the Omni on November 20. I'm all for Santa. And I'm even more for eggnog. I will not strike a dark note at a Christmas party. Out there, I hope that you too will fa-la-la with the best of them. But in here, inside the walls of Christ Church, it is not Christmas yet. It is Advent. And make no mistake—Advent begins in the dark. And be forewarned, this is an Advent sermon; hence, it is a dark sermon.

We have just prayed, "Almighty God, give us grace to cast away the works of darkness." The passage from Romans 13 also talks about the "works of darkness." In our reading from Matthew, Jesus speaks about the Son of Man returning like a thief in the dark of night. And our reading from Isaiah, from which I will be preaching, looks to a time when the darkness will be cast away, urging us to "walk in the light of the LORD!"

In the Bible, as in most works of literature, darkness is an obvious metaphor for blindness, for sin, for lostness, confusion, and despair. Ironically, the darkness of the world is easy to see on every level. As G. K. Chesterton once said, original sin "is the only part of Christian theology which can really be proved." All you have to do is look around.

We get the *Economist* magazine every week. We like it because it gives us a short but thorough tour of the world's news. Sadly, the weekly world tour is almost always a dark one. For instance, the most recent issue reports fighting in Bangladesh, bird flu in Hong Kong, hundreds trampled to death in Cambodia, the collapse of Ireland's economy due to greedy bankers, and the ever-present violence in the Middle East. And that is just the first column of the first page. The "works of darkness" are all around.

But of course, you don't have to read the *Economist* or even look outward to see the works of darkness. All I have to do is look at my own dark heart. It is easy to see the judgment and the criticism that live there. It is easy to see the lust and the anger that live there. It is easy to see the fear and the unbelief that live there. To "cast off the works of darkness" would be to evict so much of what so comfortably inhabits my dark heart.

Original sin may be the only doctrine we can prove, but I find that people violently resist its claims. *Lord of the Flies* was deeply criticized for being too dark, for taking too negative a view of human nature. You hear it all the time—whenever you call somebody a "good person"—*oh, he is a good person, she is a good person, those people in the heartland, they are just good people.* Jesus *clearly* says in the Bible that *nobody* is good except God alone. That quote does remind me of my current favorite lawyer joke.

> Q: When lawyers die, why are they buried 12 feet rather than 6 feet under the ground?

> A: Because deep down they are really good people!

I remember talking with a very secular and accomplished young woman about the dark human heart, making honest references to my own dark heart and the difficulty of love in any marriage, including my own. I thought that maybe I had gotten through to her, for the sake of the Gospel. A week or so later I asked her brother what she thought of our talk. He laughed and said, "Paul, she is worried about you. She thinks you have self-esteem problems and that your marriage is falling apart!"

Last summer I presided over a wedding in a spectacularly beautiful setting in the mountains of Vermont. The bride and groom were both spectacularly beautiful and accomplished people, as were all their family and friends. It was 68 degrees with no humidity; cows were peacefully lowing in the distance. The hills were alive with the sound of music and the language of love.

I then got up and preached a sermon about their dark hearts and their inability to love each other in their own strength and how no spouse is ultimately trustworthy in himself or herself. Their only hope was to be found in Jesus Christ. Well, what a buzz kill! Wasn't I the fly in the punch bowl. Nobody talked to me the entire reception. Even my wife Christie got up and moved to another table! At least the food was good.

Who really wants to hear the Bible's news that the works of darkness that need to be cast off originate in our own hearts? Most people believe that deep down we are really good people and that all we need is a little education, a little life coaching, a little positive thinking.

Well, to that argument, I would posit *Lord of the Flies,* the *Economist* magazine, an honest tour through your own heart, the clear and plain words of Jesus Christ, and the gruesome witness of century after bloody century. History cries out against us: we cannot successfully govern ourselves. Yes, thankfully, there are pockets of success. There are instances of peace. But, in the end, we are like 13-year-old boys stranded on a dark island in need of light and rescue. That's why I would never leave a young couple heading into marriage leaning on their own devices. What a cruel thing to do.

Give us grace to cast away the works of darkness. The Bible is clear about where the darkness comes from. We live in darkness when we refuse to be governed by God. We live in darkness when we do not accept God's authority over our lives. We live in darkness when we believe that we are our own judges. This is the essence of original sin.

This is what Paul says in Romans: "though they knew God, they did not honor him as God or give thanks to him, but they became futile in their thinking, and their senseless minds were darkened." So-called freedom from God's authority leads not to freedom but to tyranny. It leads to Nietzsche's will to power. It leads to violence and the subjection of the weak and the powerless. It leads to foolish and darkened hearts. Ultimately, it leads us to the darkness of hell.

To be delivered from darkness, we need someone to rescue us, to govern us, to bring us light. In the words of Isaiah, we need someone to "teach us his ways ... that we may walk in his paths." We need someone to "judge between the nations" and "arbitrate for many peoples." We need someone who will make us "beat [our] swords into plowshares, and [our] spears into pruning hooks"—even the swords we use against those who are closest to us.

Advent begins in the dark and yearns for the light. Advent aches for the day when we shall not learn war anymore. As we pray today, Advent yearns for "the last day, when Jesus Christ shall come in his glorious majesty to judge both the living and the dead." And when he comes, we shall sob. Sob with relief at his return. Sob with humiliation and sadness at what we have done to one another. But he shall not turn away to let us get ourselves together. He shall gather us up in his arms, with laughter in his eyes, and rise with us to the life immortal. And our dark hearts will no longer be dark. Our deepest desire will be to be ruled by him, who rules with grace. We will love him because he has loved us.

We may long for his judgment and his authority because he once visited us in great humility. The darkness of your heart beckoned him, and he came for you. We who are baptized into him may long for him from the darkness. Why? The words of a French Reformed baptismal liturgy express it best:

> For you, little child, Jesus Christ has come, he has fought, he has suffered. For you he entered the shadow of Gethsemane and the horror of Calvary. For you he uttered the cry "It is finished!" For you he rose from the dead and ascended into heaven and there he intercedes—for you, little child, even though you do not know it. But in this way the word of the Gospel becomes true. "We love him, because he first loved us."

Amen.

November 27, 2011 ‡ *First Sunday of Advent (B)*

Cheer Up, Sleepy Jean

MARK 13:24-37

My wife and I were at a funeral reception not long ago. Christie was sitting on a sofa next to a 94-year-old man named Uncle Boo, whose wonderful 101-year-old sister had just died. Uncle Boo was having a grand old time, having a drink, eating his cheese and cracker, sitting in his niece's beautiful living room.

At 94, a little bit of confusion had set in, but still, there he was. After an hour or so, Uncle Boo turned to Christie and said, "You know? I'd be having a lot more fun if I knew where I was and who it was that brought me here!"

I'm not so sure about Uncle Boo's comment. He seemed to be having a good enough time as it was. And the more I think about it, there are plenty of times when you might be having a much better time if you didn't know where you were or who brought you! It may be better not to be alert from time to time.

In the Gospel reading on this first Sunday of Advent, Jesus tells his listeners to keep alert: "Beware ... be on the watch ... keep awake." Why must we be so vigilant?

Well, Advent begins with watching and waiting, with staying awake. Not just waiting for Christmas, but watching and waiting for the Lord's return. In today's passage, especially the second part, Jesus talks about his Second Coming or, as we prayed in our collect, "the last day, when he shall come again in his glorious majesty to judge both the living and the dead." We are to keep awake and watch for his return. We are to be like servants waiting for the master of the house to return after a long journey. He didn't say when he was going to return, but we need to be on the lookout.

No one knows when this will happen, but we know that it will happen. This is what we affirm in our communion prayer when we say, "Christ has died, Christ is risen, Christ will come again." But nobody knows when this "Day of the Lord" will take place.

Many people talk about it and prognosticate about it and plan for it. Many people even predict the date and time of the Day of the Lord. They line up the texts from Revelation with the current events in the Middle East and they say that Jesus will come again within the year, or in 2017, or within the next 50 years.

Biblically speaking, all that kind of talk is nonsense. Jesus himself says, "about that day or hour no one knows, neither the angels in heaven, nor the Son, but only the Father." So if anyone tells you that he has read the signs and warns that you'll be "left behind" if you don't get on the train now, then just tell him to go read his Bible.

So yes, Advent reminds us to stay awake and keep alert. But I want to go in a different direction in this Advent sermon. Because Advent sermons that focus on waiting and watching for the Second Coming have always depressed me. I've preached plenty of them myself and have depressed myself with my own sermons. The image I conjure of waiting is not a good one.

I get terribly anxious when I'm waiting and watching, especially when I'm waiting and watching for Christie. When she's out and I'm home and she's late, I get extremely anxious. I pace around and look out the windows every five seconds. I yell at the kids to turn the television down. I'm just sure that she's gotten into a fatal car accident. I listen for a helicopter flying overhead to the hospital, wait for a call from the police. I start planning life without her, and I'm just miserable. All of this happens in a span of about three minutes. I just can't help it.

Is it rational? Of course not, although sadly we know these things can and do happen. But do I know that when Christie is with someone she forgets all about time? Yes, and it's one of the things I love about her. But that doesn't have any effect on my anxiety. I could call her cell phone—*if she had a cell phone!* I'm pretty sure the main reason she doesn't have a cell phone is because I would be calling her all the time.

So that's my image of waiting, watching for the Lord's return. The command to stay awake isn't much better. It's kind of an impossible command! When you're reading after dinner and really want to stay awake, you just can't. It's like you are getting hypnotized: "You are getting very sleepy ..." Then you wake up 30 minutes later, book open the same page, glasses askew, mouth open, maybe a little bit of drool. Not a pretty sight.

And trying to sleep when you can't sleep is way worse. Anybody who struggles with insomnia knows the cruelty of the night. You are exhausted, there is nothing you'd rather do than sleep, you'd give your kingdom for just six uninterrupted hours of shut-eye, and you just lie awake, your mind racing, your dread growing.

An article in the *New York Times* a few weeks ago called prescription sleeping pills the new "mother's little helper." Nearly 3 in 10 American women fessed up to using some kind of sleep aid at least a few nights a week. One interviewee admitted to taking Xanax, an anti-anxiety medication, a few nights a week. But she worries about addiction, so some nights, rather than taking it, she just doesn't sleep at all. She sees "the irony in not sleeping because she was anxious about taking an anti-anxiety medicine in order to sleep."

The point of talking about sleep and the lack thereof is that sometimes you just have no control over staying awake or falling asleep. Even drugs sometimes don't do the trick. Sleep is one of God's built-in indicators that you are not always in control. So if we're judged by Jesus command to stay awake, especially after 2000 years of waiting for him to return, then we aren't doing too well. Maybe that's why waiting and watching sermons never go over very well.

There must be something more here in this Advent passage. Yes, of course it is true that we wait for the Lord to return, even long for the Day when he will come, and all hurt and suffering and sorrow will come to an end. But we need a little something now, don't we?

And by golly, we do have a little something *now*—more than

a little something. In the first part of today's passage, Jesus says, "From the fig tree learn its lesson: as soon as its branch becomes tender and puts forth its leaves, you know that summer is near. So also, when you see these things taking place, you know that he is near, at the very gates. Truly I tell you, this generation will not pass away until all these things have taken place."

Did you catch that? *This* generation—Jesus' generation—will not pass away until these things have taken place. Jesus is talking about something big happening, and happening right in their midst. It could be the destruction of the Temple, which happened in AD 70, before that generation passed away. But he's also talking about himself, his own destruction, which would happen in just a few short days.

Yes, Jesus will come again. But in his death and resurrection we already have the whole story and nothing less—the "full, perfect, and sufficient sacrifice, oblation, and satisfaction for the sins of the whole world," as we say in our prayer book. Yes, he will come again, but "since no one, not even [Jesus], knows beans about the timing of that day, nothing counts now but our trust that, in him, everything is already fulfilled." So cheer up, sleepy Jean! Yes, he's coming again, but yes, he's already here.

"Keep awake," Jesus says in today's Gospel. He said it again just a few days later, and again and again—three times, in fact, as he was sweating blood in the Garden of Gethsemane: "He came and found [the disciples] sleeping; and he said to Peter, 'Simon, are you asleep? Could you not keep awake one hour?'" No, they couldn't, just like me. And guess what? He went and died for them anyway, for all of us who couldn't and can't stay awake like we ought to. Jesus stayed awake for us.

"[K]eep alert," Jesus said. Many of us, if truth be told, don't really know where we are or who brought us here. I'll tell you the answer to that question this first Sunday of Advent. You are a sinner saved by grace, and you've been brought into this house of forgiveness by your Savior who "will neither slumber nor sleep," but keeps watch over you, the one he loves.

Amen.

December 24, 2005 ‡ *Christmas Eve*

Born in Bedlam

LUKE 2:1-14

Welcome and Merry Christmas. What compares to the electricity in the air at a crowded Christmas Eve service?

You might be a Christ Church regular with all your very wired and fidgety kids—welcome. (Don't worry: 5 pm Christmas Eve sermons are short and well amplified.) You might be out-of-town family—welcome. You might be a first-time visitor—welcome. You might be part of the famous C-and-E crowd (Christmas and Easter Christians)—double welcome to you. We're just thrilled that you're all here to hear again about this baby born in Bethlehem.

Because of this baby born in Bethlehem, Christianity itself is a place of welcome. It's not a club for the good or the religious or the pious or the moral. Because of the baby born in Bethlehem, Christianity is *the* place of welcome for one and all, and especially for the ones who can't seem to be good or religious or pious or moral.

You know who I mean: the ones who yelled at their kids on the way over here, the ones who are really relieved that the difficult sister isn't coming to dinner this year, the ones who are more interested in getting than giving, or the ones who like to give only to be thanked and appreciated.

Here, tonight at Christ Church, is the place of welcome for one and all: the all-together and the anxious, the workers and the worried, the joyful and the jaded, the believers and the bored. Christianity is the place where you come as you are and not as you think you should be.

One of the good things about Christmas Eve is that there will be no more Christmas catalogues coming in the mail, which have been arriving since late September, and no more Christmas issues of gorgeous magazines. These catalogues and magazines make me feel terrible. They show me Christmas as I think it should be. They present an image of Christmas in which everybody is beautiful and happy and glad to see one another. Everything is in place and dripping with understated but perfect yuletide taste.

L.L.Bean shows you the golden retriever puppies in front of the fire, but leaves out the dog hair on the carpet. Lands' End shows you happy children in front of a Christmas tree calmly opening presents, but doesn't show you the greed, jealousy, disappointment, or entitlement that is provoked by an iPod or a Groovy Girls doll—or the wrong colored iPod or last year's Groovy Girls doll. You get the picture: life as it actually is, usually some form of bedlam, especially at this time of the year.

Of course, you don't have to have children to know this problem. You just have to have a roommate or a mother or a co-worker or any other living human being. There is always some kind of relational bedlam going on with somebody, even if it's just with yourself. You might not feel that going home for Christmas is like walking into a "circular firing squad" as one student told me recently, but every family has its serious dysfunctions. Divorce, disease, and death make sure of that. There's an empty chair this year, or because of cancer there will be one next year. There's a child with the other parent because it's their turn this Christmas.

And, of course, the tensions and stresses and alienation and anxiety in families is a microcosm of the world itself, of the family of nations at war with one another. A look at the paper gives you a view of the bedlam that is always a constant in global human life.

Whatever your form of bedlam—and maybe by the grace of God it is held at bay—you've come tonight to hear about the baby born at Bethlehem. What does his entrance into the human theater mean to us?

Our bishop, Peter Lee, shared the etymology of the word bedlam in his Christmas letter this year. Bedlam denotes chaos and anxiety. The word actually comes from a medieval mental asylum in London named St. Mary of Bethlehem. In London slang "Bethlehem" was shortened to "bedlam." How right on. That, of course is the heart of the Christmas message. Jesus Christ was born in Bethlehem. Jesus Christ was born in *bedlam*. Jesus came and comes into life as it actually is. He comes into your life as it actually is.

The first Christmas could never be in a catalogue or magazine. Joseph and Mary were homeless refugees, fleeing an oppressive government. Mary was an unwed teen mother with no insurance. The baby was born on the run, in a stable, away from friends and family, without midwives or attention or drugs.

The Bible says it this way: "And she brought forth her firstborn son, and wrapped him in swaddling clothes, and laid him in a manger; because there was no room for them in the inn."

Talk about bedlam. Giving birth in a barn after riding a donkey on the lam? Even the beautiful King James language can't entirely obfuscate the chaos and anxiety that must have been present in the scene.

Jesus Christ born in bedlam. What does this mean for you? It means that your life doesn't have to look like an L.L.Bean catalogue for Jesus to come into it. He comes into your life as it is. He is born in bedlam. As Bishop Lee says so beautifully, "what we celebrate at Christmas and what draws the crowds is the message that in the midst of human life as it is, with homeless people, a disordered world, with frustration and sadness and loneliness, Christ is born and boundless hope and joy enter the human experience."

That's the extraordinary and beautiful news of Christmas. It's what makes Christianity a place of welcome for all comers, especially the weary and heavy-laden, as the baby will say later when he grows up. Bedlam is our life, and Jesus is born straight into it.

Why not turn to him this Christmas, even right now, with all the bedlam in your life, with all the pain and the loss and the strain and the breakage. Why not "come and adore him"? He loves you even and especially in your bedlam. He was born in it and born for it.

Sure, there is also joy and order and happiness, and I pray that your Christmas is full of those things. But for those here who feel the bedlam in your family or the world, then hear again the short and well-amplified message of the Christmas angel: "Fear not: for, behold, I bring you good tidings of great joy, which shall be to all people. For unto you is born this day in the city of David"—the city of Bethlehem, the city of Bedlam—"a Saviour, which is Christ the Lord."

Merry Christmas and Amen.

January 3, 2010 ‡ *Epiphany*

Birth or Death?

MATTHEW 2:1-12

A cold coming they had of it at this time of the year, just the worst time of the year to take a journey, and specially a long journey. The ways deep, the weather sharp, ... "the very dead of winter."

You may feel like this is a description of trying to get to church or work or anywhere else since the snow came two weeks ago. It is in fact a sermon that Anglican Bishop Lancelot Andrewes preached in 1622 to King James in Christmastide.

It is also how T. S. Eliot begins his poem about today's Gospel reading—the account of the "Journey of the Magi." The poem is narrated by one of the wise men at the end of his life, reflecting on their journey from the East, under the direction of the star, to pay homage to Jesus with their gifts of gold, frankincense, and myrrh.

Scripture says that once the wise men finally found Jesus they "rejoiced with exceeding great joy." The journey was worth it, despite the discomfort and frustration, as Eliot narrated them.

The travel from points East was arduous. The Bible doesn't say exactly where the Magi came from, who they were, or even how many there were. Later tradition numbered them three, and later Christians called them kings, interpreting some Old Testament passages through the lens of the Incarnation. We surmise that these men were learned, wealthy, and pagan; they could have come from Iraq or Afghanistan or Pakistan. We do not know.

What we do know is that the Magi followed a star, which came to rest over the newborn King. And when that star finally led them to Jesus, the Magi "saw the young child with Mary his mother, and fell down, and worshipped him." In Eliot's poem, one wise man's encounter with Jesus changed his life forever, as any real encounter with God will do. For this reason, the wise man says of the difficult journey, "I would do it again."

The wise man would do it again, but in his reflection on his encounter with Jesus, he asks a poignant question: "were we led all that way for / Birth or Death?" What a question. What does it mean?

As we've just said, once the wise man encountered Jesus Christ, the true and only God, his life was changed. He could no longer go back to his old pagan ways. His old self had to die. Hence the birth of Christ became his own death.

The wise man says that that Birth was "our death":

> We returned to our places, these Kingdoms,
> But no longer at ease here, in the old dispensation,
> With an alien people clutching their gods.

What the Magi and Eliot and the Bible are saying is that once you have met and worshiped Jesus Christ, the only Son of the Father and the God of Grace, then you can never really be at home in the world, in your old life. As the scripture says, once the Magi met Jesus, "they departed into their own country *another way.*"

The old dispensation is filled with people trying to look out for themselves, justify themselves, prove themselves. The old dispensation is filled with greed and abuse and the glory of the self. But an encounter with Jesus Christ must result in what the Bible calls death to self. If there is to be a birth for us, there must be a death for us.

What this death looks like for people is both exactly alike and totally different. It is exactly alike in that every worshiper of Jesus must die to his own agenda for his life. Every believer must die to her own claim to control. Every Christian must die to his own illusions of self-sovereignty. If you are claimed by Jesus Christ, then "you were bought with a price"; "you are not your own."

So it's all the same for you, me, and the Magi. But this Death is different for each one of us, because it will take a different shape depending on your circumstances. It may mean accepting your limitations. It may mean dying to your career hopes. It may mean giving up on romance. It may mean moving to Haiti to work with orphans.

And it may mean doing exactly the life you've been given to do but doing it out of an entirely different motivation: that is, living for God and not living for self. Once you have met Jesus Christ, you may return to your own country, but always by *another way*.

C. S. Lewis writes about the totality of this death to self and this life to God:

> Christ says "Give me All. I don't want so much of your time and so much of your money and so much of your work: I want You. I have not come to torment your natural self, but to kill it. No half-measures are any good. I don't want to cut off a branch here and a branch there, I want to have the whole tree down. I don't want to drill the tooth, or crown it, or stop it, but to have it out. Hand over the whole natural self, all the desires which you think innocent as well as the ones you think wicked—the whole outfit. I will give you a new self instead. In fact, I will give you Myself: my own will shall become yours."

Lewis is exactly right on God's total demand, our death to self. As the baby born in a stable would say when he grew up, "unless a grain of wheat falls into the earth and dies, it remains just a single grain; but if it dies, it bears much fruit." But the command to hand over the whole natural self—which is the only way to real life—is an impossible one, isn't it? Or if you hand it over, don't you find that you keep clutching it back, along with your gods?

Our wills are too weak to just hand it all over, even though we know that this is the way to real life. The failure of the will hits home for most people around New Year's resolution time. I saw a great benediction the other day: "May your troubles last only as long as your New Year's resolutions!" As Scripture says, "the spirit is willing, but the flesh is weak."

I recently visited with a woman who is about turn 100 years old. Her daughter and I asked her to tell us her secret to long life. She replied, "Good clean living and plenty of bourbon." She paused and then continued, "Now by good clean living, I don't mean it has to be immaculate." That's good news, because none of us comes anywhere close to immaculate living.

But there was one who lived an immaculate life for our sake. This is why we are called to a life of trust, not in ourselves, but in God. We trust not only in his life for our life, but also his death for our death to self. As we often say here: Jesus lived the life for us that we could never live, and Jesus died the death for us that we deserved to die. And his life and his death are reckoned to us through faith and trust.

Or as we say in the 1928 version of our prayer of humble access, we come to God not "trusting in our own righteousness, but in thy manifold and great mercies." Through our trust in his birth and his death for us, "our sinful bodies may be made clean by his body, and our souls washed through his most precious blood."

The Magi discovered that in Jesus' birth was his death, that in his newborn body lay the blood that would be shed for them and for all humankind. You might know that the gift of myrrh brought by the Magi to the baby Jesus was a gift signaling the cross. As we sing in our famous Epiphany hymn,

> Myrrh is mine; it's bitter perfume
> Breathes a life of gathering gloom;
> Sorrowing, sighing, bleeding, dying,
> Sealed in the stone-cold tomb.

Our death to self—and make no mistake: your death to self is the only way to real life—is bound up entirely in his death for self, for your self. For as Scripture says, "If we have died with him, we will also live with him." Jesus, born for us, crucified for us, and raised for us, says to you today and always, "I will give you a new self instead. In fact, I will give you Myself."

Amen.

January 9, 2010 ‡ *First Sunday after Epiphany (A)*

The Voice

MATTHEW 3:13-17

This morning we read about Jesus' baptism in the Jordan River. John baptizes Jesus, and as Jesus emerges from the water a voice from heaven says, "This is my Son, the Beloved, with whom I am well pleased."

Last week there was an article in the *Wall Street Journal* about another kind of voice. The article was about a new therapeutic approach to address the ongoing array of human dysfunction: the voices of fear, anxiety, and self-condemnation that accuse us from within. You know what I'm talking about: all the loud and destructive tenants that take up residence in your head without paying rent. The article begins:

> The boss loves your work. Your spouse thinks you're sexy. The kids—and even the cat—shower you with affection. But then there's the Voice, the nagging presence in your head that tells you you're a homely, heartless slacker.
>
> Even people who appear supremely fit, highly successful and hyper-organized are sometimes riddled with debilitating doubts, fears, and self-criticisms.

The writer of the article capitalizes the V in Voice. The Voice seems to have an ontology all its own. This is not a new idea, of course. Who is not aware of the near constant murmur of condemnation? Maybe you are not given to obvious self-criticism, but there are different forms of the Voice.

For instance, do you know anyone who is always justifying herself? Or do you know anyone who is always bragging about himself? Self-justification and self-aggrandizement are forms of the same Voice, just spoken from a different place. If you keep telling yourself, and others, of course, how great you are, or what you have done to deserve whatever it is you think you deserve, then you might begin to believe it.

I loved the old *Saturday Night Live* character named Stuart Smalley, a needy self-help talk-show host. He would begin each day by looking in the mirror and repeating his "ILACs": "I am Lovable And Capable, and goshdarnit, people like me!" Then by the end of the show he would always dissolve in tears and self-recrimination.

Usually, the Voice just speaks for itself, telling you that you are not good enough, skinny enough, funny enough, smart enough, disciplined enough, or doing enough. To the Voice, we wish to say, "Enough already!"

Sometimes the Voice becomes the voices of those around us, those who are close to us. There is a now-famous episode of *Seinfeld* about the alternative holiday called "Festivus," "the holiday for the rest of us." George Costanza's family celebrated Festivus each December 23. Festivus traditions including "Feats of Strength" and "The Airing of Grievances."

At dinner, George's father gathers everyone around the table for the Airing of Grievances and declares, "I've got a lot of problems with you people, and now you're going to hear about all of them!" Turning to his son, he yells, "You're weak, George! You're just weak!"

Funny how a Family Festivus and a Family Christmas are sometimes not that different. Just after Christmas, I spoke to one son whose father sat him down and told him what a disappointing son he was. Just before Christmas, I spoke with a father whose grown son emailed to tell him what a disappointing father he was. And all during Christmas, I'm wondering if I've been a good enough son and a good enough father!

As W. H. Auden says in the post-Christmas section of his poem *For the Time Being*, after the holidays, we find that we have

> attempted—quite unsuccessfully—
> To love all our relatives, and in general
> Grossly overestimated our powers.

The Voice. "You're weak, George!" Where does the Voice come from and what can we do to silence It? The answer is a little complicated. But one part of the Voice is in fact true and accurate. This is the Voice of the Law—God's standard for our lives. Each of us has failed to meet God's standard, so we feel justly accused. If you believe that you have met the standards of God's Law, then you have grossly overestimated your powers. George is, in fact, weak.

As theologian Gerhard Forde says, the Voice rises "from the demands which society makes upon us, the demands of family and friends and the voices and faces of suffering humanity. ... And above all it is the command of God that we must love him with all our heart, and our neighbor as ourselves." Remember, Jesus says, "Be perfect, therefore, as your heavenly Father is perfect." How's that working for you?

Because one part of the Voice is rooted in truth—that we are indeed guilty of failing to love God and to love our neighbor—then we will never be successful in stopping the Voice by our ILACs, by plain self-affirmation, by telling ourselves over and over again that we are lovable and capable. You know this from your own experience.

You will not be able to silence the Voice yourself. It is also true that others will not be able to silence it for you. Those of us who need affirmation from others—and believe me, "words of affirmation" are one of my "Five Love Languages"—will tell you that affirmation comes and goes like smoke through a keyhole. It finds its way in, feels good for a moment, and then dissipates into thin air, leaving you in the same needy place you were before, listening against your will to the Voice telling you you're a homely, heartless slacker.

If we cannot silence the Voice, and those around us cannot

silence the Voice, then who can silence the Voice? We obviously need another Voice, a stronger Voice, a deeper Voice to speak to us. I said earlier that the other accusing voice is in part true. But, there is also another, truer Voice. It is the same Voice that once said to Jesus, "This is my Son, the Beloved, with whom I am well pleased."

If the accusing Voice is the Voice of the Law, then the deeper and truer Voice is the Voice of the Gospel. And the Gospel is this: what God says to Jesus, God says to you. You are my son; with you I am well pleased. You are my daughter; with you I am well pleased.

Given what you know about yourself and maybe what you did yesterday or imagined doing the day before, this Voice may be hard to believe. That's the devil's job, by the way—the father of lies telling you that the truer voice is not true at all, that the Gospel is nothing but psychological smoke and mirrors.

The Voice of accusation only stops when the Law has been fulfilled: when we do live the perfect life, when we do love God with all our heart, when we do love our relatives quite successfully, when we are entirely lovable and entirely capable. Although we can never fulfill the Law, Jesus Christ has fulfilled it for us.

It is interesting that God says that he is well pleased with Jesus, even before his first miracle, his first sermon, his first healing. God says he is well pleased with Jesus long before his death on the cross for the forgiveness of our sins. In the same way, God say to you that you please him, despite the evidence to the contrary.

The reality of life with sin being what it is, the devil being who he is, and humans being what we are, the voice of accusation will never be fully silenced this side of heaven. Life sometimes seems like a continual Airing of Grievances followed by endless Feats of Strength. But it is also true, as the Bible says, that "Christ is the end of the law." In other words, Christ is the end of the Voice. For those who trust in Christ, there is a new sheriff in town.

"He that hath an ear, let him hear." May we all have ears to hear. At least for the time being.

Amen.

January 23, 2011 ‡ *Third Sunday after Epiphany (A)*

Grace Is Foolish

1 COR 1:10-18

I n our "Grace in Practice" adult education class last week, Dave Zahl commented on the growing 3D craze in the movie industry. It's a racket for sure; you pay five dollars more and in return get a pair of silly looking glasses with opposing lenses, one blue and one red. The lenses work in tension with each other to create the three-dimensional experience.

Our country is no stranger to tension, especially red and blue tension. This morning I want to talk about a tension that has existed from the beginning—opposing points of view that operate in all of life. I'm talking about Law and grace, which are just theological code words for the tension between demand and acceptance, criticism and approval, judgment and love. This tension flows throughout everything we do. One lens is the Law, the other lens of grace.

As Paul Zahl says in the beginning of *Grace in Practice*, "In life there are two governing principles that are at war with one another. ... So powerful are these principles, so virile and unquenchable, so captivating and irresistible, that all relationships, all human operations, simply lie down before them. The law crushes the human spirit; grace lifts it."

We see Law and grace in dramatic tension in Paul's First Letter to the Corinthians. So much so that the message of grace is received as utter foolishness, as nonsensical talk by those who live by Law. Grace has no place in a grown-up world that prizes wisdom and education and prowess, along with the spoils that go to the victors. The tension is so great that Paul describes it as life and death. If the word of the cross (grace and forgiveness) is folly to you, then you are one who does and will perish; if the word of the cross is your lifeline in a world of Law, then you are one who is and will be saved.

Let me talk about this tension between Law and grace through illustration rather than assertion. It is always illustration or story, rather than assertion, that brings a truth home. This is why Jesus told so many stories and why he usually refused to answer any question in a clear, plainspoken way. So here we go.

By now you may have heard of the Yale law professor named Amy Chua who, in response to what she perceives as an epidemic of lackadaisical parenting in America, wrote a book called *Battle Hymn of the Tiger Mother*. As the *New York Times Magazine* says, "in contrast to the flaccid, touchy-feely Western variety" of parenting which emphasizes building self-esteem through praise, Chua endorses Chinese parenting which "stresses respect, self-discipline, and, above all, results."

I must say, in the roller coaster that is parenting, I'm all for respect, self-discipline, and results. Especially when we are feeling out of control, Christie and I tend to "lay down the law." This is why *Tiger Mother* has struck a chord. But Chua has made herself public enemy number one among parents everywhere by her version of the Law: she is all demand. And the children better produce perfectly. No "foolishness" will be tolerated.

For instance, Chua pushes her children to get straight A's and forces them to spend hours a day practicing piano and violin. They are not allowed to play the drums, which "leads to drugs." When her 4-year-old daughter Lulu presents her with a birthday card, her mother judges that it couldn't have taken "more than 20 seconds" to make, so she declares, "I want a better one—one that you've put some thought and effort into. ... I deserve better than this. So I *reject* this."

Extreme example. But, then again, the Law is extreme. Jesus says in the Sermon on the Mount, "unless your righteousness exceeds that of the scribes and Pharisee"—and perhaps the drummers?—"you will never enter the kingdom of heaven." That is the magnifying lens of the Law.

In contrast, Langston Hughes wrote a touching short story seen through the lens of grace, called "Thank you, M'am." A boy tries to steal the purse of a woman, but the strap breaks and the boy falls and the woman grabs hold of the boy:

> "If I turn you loose, will you run?" asked the woman.
> "Yes'm," said the boy.
> "Then I won't turn you loose," said the woman.
>
> ...
>
> "Was I bothering you when I turned that corner?"
> "No'm."
> "But, you put yourself in contact with me," said the woman. "If you think that that contact is not going to last awhile, you got another thought coming. When I get through with you, sir, you are going to remember Mrs. Luella Bates Washington Jones."
> Sweat popped out on the boy's face and he began to struggle. Mrs. Jones stopped, jerked him around in front of her, put a half nelson about his neck, and continued to drag him up the street. When she got to her door, she dragged the boy inside, down a hall, and into a large kitchenette-furnished room at the rear of the house. ... The woman still had him by the neck in the middle of her room.

At this point you think Luella is going to turn into a ferocious Tiger Mother. But then the story shifts. She makes the boy wash his dirty face and starts making a meal for him. He must have been hungry, she assumes, since he wanted her money. Seeing her generous response, he feels able to speak more candidly: "'I wanted a pair of blue suede shoes,' said the boy."

The boy, now free, has the chance to make a dash for it. But he doesn't. He stays as Luella cooks him supper. She tells him,

> "I were young once and I wanted things I could not get."
> There was another long pause. The boy's mouth opened. Then he frowned, but not knowing he frowned.

The woman said, "Um-hum! You thought I was going to say but didn't you? You thought I was going to say, *but I didn't snatch people's pocketbooks.* Well, I wasn't going to say that. ... I have done things, too, which I would not tell you, son— neither tell God, if He didn't already know. So you set down while I fix us something to eat."

The story ends with Luella giving the boy 10 dollars to buy himself some blue suede shoes.

I'll speak personally for a moment. It was not until my wife and I discovered the grace of God in its fullness 10 years ago—five years after I was ordained and 20 years after a conversion to Christiani- ty—that our lives really changed for the better. Grace has made me into a husband who is loved by his wife because grace has enabled me to be a husband who loves his wife and a person who loves oth- ers. It has changed the way we treat our children, our "careers," and our money. For us who are being saved by grace, it is the power of God. I am beyond grateful that God, like Luella Bates Washing- ton Jones, put himself in contact with me.

As a minister, most people expect me to say a "but" when I preach the grace of God: "God's grace is free, but you better not take advantage of it." Or, "God loves you as you are, but you really need to start behaving better." Well, I am not going to say that, and the Gospel never will say that. And I have done things, too, which I would not tell you—or God, if he didn't already know. Much better to "proclaim the Gospel" as Paul says today, and then have every- body just sit down and eat.

Two lenses through which to see the world: the lens of the Law and the lens of grace. And to be sure, you need both lenses. 3D glasses don't work with just one lens. God's Law is good; it is right for children to have discipline and respect. There is no grace with- out Law. John says in the prologue to his Gospel, "The law came through Moses; grace and truth came through Jesus Christ."

The Law cannot produce what it commands. It may produce a better birthday card, but that birthday card will be presented with the clutched fist of resentment. You know this from your experi- ence. Jesus Christ came to show us one thing for sure: only grace can really change a heart. And he did not just tell us; he showed us.

The word of the cross is the Word made flesh on the cross.

What a foolish way for God to act. To come, be ridiculed, and then to perish for a world that thinks he and his ways are foolish. Grace is clearly for the foolish; for those who are content to be doormats. Well, Jesus, in his graceful foolishness is a doormat, stepped on by all to welcome you into heaven. For us who are being saved, it is the power of God.

Amen.

January 27, 2013 ‡ *Third Sunday after Epiphany (C)*

A Postponed Ceremony Accommodates the Naked Person

LUKE 4:14-21

I recently heard a true story about a minister who sent an urgent message to everyone in his church: "No matter what you are doing, no matter what your excuse, no matter what you have to cancel to make it happen, make sure you are at church on Sunday, January 20." As you might imagine, this created all kinds of wonder and anticipation among the congregation. On the appointed Sunday morning, the church was standing-room only.

When it was time for the sermon, the minister ascended the pulpit. People were on the edge of their seats. The eyes of all the church were fixed upon him. What special word from God would he have for them? Instead, the minister proceeded to rip into the congregation. He chastised them for their irregular church attendance. He challenged the sincerity of their faith:

> Why can you take your children without fail to cotillion or to lacrosse tournaments but cannot take them to youth group? Why can you afford a country club but not afford to tithe to the church? Where is your commitment? How do you expect to get anything out of the church or your faith if you won't put anything into it? God is faithful to do his part,

but you know that you must do your part.

And with several other such harangues the minister reduced the congregation to tears with guilt and shame.

The immediate effect on the congregation was increased attendance and higher giving. Guilt works well in the short run. But after a few months, of course, everyone settled back into the status quo. That's because guilt and recrimination can never affect lasting change.

The minister probably thought that the Lord had called him to preach a prophetic sermon to convict the lukewarm masses. He was probably encouraged to do so by some eager staff and vestry members. He was likely congratulated for his courage and moral vision. After all, he was doing his duty to right the rails of the congregation that had clearly lost its way. He was the captain and it was up to him to right the ship.

This is the way the world thinks. We all know this. But this is not the way the Gospel thinks. From the Gospel perspective, it was not the congregation that had lost its way; it was the minister who had lost his way. Not that I can't sympathize with his frustrations. But the Christian minister had abandoned his calling. He had turned the church into a lecture hall and the pulpit into a judge's bench. At his ordination he was set apart as an evangelist; that Sunday he forsook his vows.

The word "evangelist" may strike you as a little cringe-worthy. That is because it has flown far away from its etymology. Evangelism has become co-terminus with a kind of wheedling moralism, usually bound up with a standard set of political causes. When you think about the guest list for your dinner party, not once does "evangelist" cross your mind.

Yet, the word "evangelist" comes from the Greek word *evange-lion*, meaning simply "good news." *Eu* means "good", and *angelion* means "news." So when a preacher gets up into a pulpit to preach, you have every right to expect "good news" rather than a tongue-lashing, a pep talk, or a to-do list for how to get your life in order.

In this morning's Gospel, Jesus gets into a pulpit for the first time in his career as a preacher. I would imagine people were on the edge of their seats. He begins by quoting Isaiah:

> The Spirit of the Lord is upon me,
> because he has anointed me
>   to bring good news to the poor.
> He has sent me to proclaim release to the captives
>   and recovery of sight to the blind,
>   to let the oppressed go free,
> to proclaim the year of the Lord's favor.

Now *that* is good news. Jesus was anointed to bring "good news." And that is all he said. After that short sermon, Jesus "rolled up the scroll, gave it back to the attendant, and sat down. The eyes of all in the synagogue were fixed on him. Then he began to say to them, 'Today this scripture has been fulfilled in your hearing.'"

Then do you know what he did? He started going to dinner parties with people who drank too much and told dirty jokes. He healed people who could not get help from respectable doctors. He helped people who had burned all their bridges. He fed people. He befriended people. There was a good reason that he was known as the "friend of sinners."

Our Christ Church group returned last week from our medical mission trip to Haiti. The non-medical types, like me, were assigned to charts and vitals. We welcomed people, took temperatures and blood pressures and weights. We recorded the information on charts for the doctors. After doing this about 80 times a day, we got fairly proficient. We joked that we should take vitals in the narthex as people come in for church. Just set up a little station back there. We thought we would take before and after church blood pressures.

Someone said that the sign of a good sermon would be a higher blood pressure after church. People need to be challenged, he said. I told him that I thought the opposite was true. You've got enough in life to raise your blood pressure. An effective sermon won't give you a to-do list to fix your life but a word of support to lower your blood pressure. It will leave you comforted and assured. That's the sure sign that you know the Gospel, the good news, has been preached.

The people of Haiti have some fabulous proverbs, many of which, for some reason, have to do with naked people. One that I don't quite understand is this: "Laugh at a short person, but not at a naked person." O.K. One that I love and think I understand is this: "A postponed ceremony accommodates the naked person."

A postponed ceremony accommodates the naked person. This means that if you don't start your event on time it really helps the people that are unprepared—the people that can't even get it together enough to put on a pair of pants! What a beautiful Gospel proverb.

Jesus says he brings good news to the unprepared. As the text says, the "poor" and the "blind" and the "captive" and the "oppressed" are unable to get prepared. They are the naked who need the ceremony postponed so they can get to it. Jesus takes it a step farther. He brings the ceremony to them, meaning that he brings the ceremony to us, who need daily help to lower our anxiety-ridden blood pressures.

The poet Christian Wiman is the editor of *Poetry* magazine. He's coming to Christ Church on March 6 to read his poetry and give a talk called "Hive of Nerves: Modern Anxiety and the Meaning of Faith." A definite not-to-be-missed event. The title poem of one of his books of poetry is called "Every Riven Thing." The recurring line is this:

"God goes belonging to every riven thing he's made."

A riven thing is a rent-apart, split-open thing, a thing broken into pieces. In the most profound way, God belongs in the riven thing because he was riven himself. His palms were riven by nails, his feet were riven by spikes, his side was riven by a spear, his brow was riven by thorns.

A riven thing is a poor, blind, captive, and oppressed thing—a thing naked and unprepared. It is a thing that needs the healing and comfort of good news and favor. The good news today and the good news every day is that "God goes belonging to every riven thing he's made." Including you.

Amen.

November 12, 2006 ‡ *Fourth Sunday after Epiphany (C)*

All That You Can't Leave Behind

1 CORINTHIANS 13

Our scripture for tonight is stunning in its power. It's probably the most famous passage in Scripture. Since love is the theme, I'm sure you've heard it at weddings over and over again. Yes, it's beautiful. But it is also widely misunderstood. To understand it, we've got to set the context. And to set the context I want to start with Ted Haggard.

Ted Haggard has been in the news. He's the now deposed pastor of a 14,000-member evangelical church and the former head of the 30-million-member National Association of Evangelicals (NAE). He was accused and has now confessed to sexual immorality and illegal drug use. Initially, Haggard denied the charges. But in his statement to his congregation last Sunday, he confessed to being "a liar and a deceiver." He confessed to his dark struggle with sexual immorality for all of his adult life. With that confession, how could you not have compassion for him? And how could you not relate to him—if not in the particulars, at least in the description of his human condition?

Apparently, the National Association of Evangelicals (NAE) could not have compassion for Haggard, nor relate to him. Leith Anderson, another megachurch pastor, has been appointed as the new NAE president. This was his statement about Haggard: "I think most evangelicals ... will understand that if there are 45,000 churches [affiliated with NAE], that 44,999 of them have leaders that did not misbehave and that one person misbehaved and that that is an anomaly."

Misbehavior is an anomaly? I guess if we want actual insight into the human condition, we have to look beyond the NAE. Perhaps we could turn to Shakespeare. I've been reading him recently. There is a reason that he is our greatest poet. Shakespeare navigates the wide terrain of human emotion with such care, pathos, and skill. He's both bawdy and profound.

I read because I want to learn but also because I want to recognize myself in what I read. Don't you? I'm particularly attuned to an author's understanding of the human heart. What does she say about the human condition? Where do I relate to his characters? How are they like me? How am I like them?

Rereading *Hamlet* has been an experience akin to worship. There are moments when I'm arrested, dead in my tracks, by Hamlet's insight into the first order questions of life—not just capital-L life, but my life. "To be or not to be" of course is the most famous. But, in Hamlet's description of himself, I find a description of me:

> I could accuse me of such things that it were better my mother had not borne me: I am very proud, revengeful, ambitious, with more offenses at my beck than I have thoughts to put them in, imagination to give them shape, or time to act them in.

This is not just a description of me but of anybody who understands the human condition in light of the Bible. Misbehavior is not an anomaly: "There is no one who is righteous, not even one." Hamlet's description of himself is true to Genesis 6: "The LORD saw that the wickedness of humankind was great in the earth, and that every inclination of the thoughts of their hearts was only evil continually."

With this kind of insight into the human heart (from Haggard, Hamlet, and Holy Scripture), reading the passage for tonight is deeply distressing. Did you feel distressed as you listened to it? Distress is not the usual emotion elicited by this famous text, often called a "Hymn to Love" and read jarringly out of context at weddings—as if Paul was interested in romantic love here. 1 Corinthians 13 has nothing to do with *eros* (romantic or sexual love) and everything to do with *agape* (selfless love for the other).

If we see this passage as *eros*—romantic or marital love—then we can feel sentimental and removed: "Love is patient; love is kind; love is not envious or boastful or arrogant or rude. It does not insist on its own way; it is not irritable or resentful; it does not rejoice in wrongdoing, but rejoices in the truth." Isn't that nice? What a lovely sentiment, dear. What a nice ideal. Let's get to the reception for a gin and tonic.

Hearing those words in the glow of nuptial sentiment is not really hearing them at all. They are not a hymn to love; they are description of love. Paul's description of love is decidedly not within the realm of human capability. And knowing our human condition, people at weddings should be weeping and wailing and repenting, on their knees begging God to give the couple what they cannot by their nature have! That would be an interesting wedding. I can read the paper's report now: "The bride was dressed in sackcloth and the groom in a hair shirt, while the wedding party groveled on the floor in conviction of sin. The reception was held at the Farmington Country Club."

Paul contrasts the perpetually misbehaving human heart with the description of the *agape* love that comes only from God. We see this in the negatives in the passage: *not* envious, *not* boastful, *not* arrogant, *not* rude, etc. Paul uses the behavior of love as a foil to typical behavior of human beings, who *are* envious, boastful, arrogant, and rude. Or as Hamlet says, "proud, revengeful, ambitious." In short, we do not have the capacity to love. Love does not rise unaided from the human heart.

As a test, insert your name where the word "love" is. Do you recognize yourself? Or do you more easily recognize yourself in the words of Hamlet or Genesis? If we hear this text and do not fall flat on our faces in light of the "thoughts of our hearts," then it is because they are too much for us to bear.

And yet! Here Paul is clearly calling the Corinthians to this *agape* love! That which we're not capable of, he's calling us to! In fact, he says that anything we do and say is entirely worthless without it! If I "do not have love, I am nothing" and "gain nothing." What a thing to say!

If I pledge a hundred grand a year, but have not love, I give nothing. If I pray everyday, go to Uganda every summer, serve the poor every Tuesday, but have not love, I gain nothing. If I preach an amazing, accurate, powerful sermon on 1 Corinthians 13, but without love, then I'm nothing but a windbag. Everything you do is worthless and hopeless without love. These are such tough standards, aren't they? That's why I felt such distress.

To hear this Scripture rightly, as we've said, is to throw yourself on the mercy of God. And, it is also to recognize not yourself in its beautiful lyric but someone else. The meaning of the text is clear when we insert another name, "the name that is above every name," the Name at which "every knee should bend ... and every tongue should confess." That is, "*Jesus* is patient; *Jesus* is kind; *Jesus* is not envious or boastful or arrogant or rude. He does not insist on its own way; he is not irritable or resentful; he does not rejoice in wrongdoing, but rejoices in the truth. He bears all things, believes all things, hopes all things, endures all things. Jesus never ends."

So how do we get this love that we do not have in our "proud, revengeful, ambitious" hearts? Well, as Fleming Rutledge says, "There is therefore a secret at the heart of this passage. *Agape* would be unattainable for the human being if it were not for God's invincible activity on our behalf, through the power of his Son's sacrifice of himself. Love does not lead to God; God in Jesus Christ leads us to love. *Agape* is not an ideal for me to aim at; *agape* is already actively at work in me from beyond myself."

We love because we have first been loved. What does this *agape*, this love that comes from being loved, look like? Think about what it is to be loved. Some of you are extremely blessed: you knew love from childhood. Others of you were deprived of love and feel your lack. Either way, you recognize love as it's described in this passage: patient, kind, enduring.

Someone who loves you puts your needs first. She thinks about what you need before you can even think of it yourself. She works behind the scenes to prepare your Halloween costume. He puts down what he's doing when you come in the room and fixes his attention on you. He listens to you pour out your day; the details he delights in, the hurts he wipes away. She has cocoa on the stove and comes to you in the night when you cry.

He loves your friends because they are your friends; she's in your corner in every case, taking your side because it is your side. At your life's end, she cares for you when you cannot care for yourself.

If you have experienced this kind of love from another person then you have experienced the hints and whispers of the love of God. You "know only in part," you "see in a mirror, dimly" the love of the One who died for the misbehaving heart. You will recognize this *agape* love from the receiving end, although you will not be aware of giving it out. For the nature of *agape* is that it is unself-conscious. It is spontaneous. It is unwitting of its goodness. When a child runs in the street in traffic, does a mother have to calculate her action? If love is forced, disciplined, chosen, or calculated, it is not love. And if you have not love, you have nothing.

But thanks be to God that *agape* is not an ideal to aim at. For those who have been loved by Jesus Christ, *agape* is already active-ly at work in us through him. That we cannot recognize it is a sure mark of its presence.

Be sure of this, love is the only thing that counts in life: "For in Christ Jesus neither circumcision nor uncircumcision counts for anything; the only thing that counts is faith working through love."

And love is the only thing that counts in the next life, too. You can't take anything else:

> You've got to leave it behind
> All that you fashion
> All that you make

But love, "it's the only baggage you can bring. / It's all that you can't leave behind."

We love because we have first been loved. We have been loved specifically, concretely, in the self-sacrifice of the One who is pa-tient and kind, the One who asked his Father to remove the bitter cup of suffering but did not insist on his own way. We have been loved by the One who bore "the sins of the whole world," and en-dured the scourge on his back, the nails in his hands and the spear in his side for our sake. We have been loved by the One whose breath and pulse ended on a Friday, but who rose again on a Sun-day rejoicing in the truth.

Amen.

February 4, 2007 ‡ *Fourth Sunday after Epiphany (B)*

Have You Come To Destroy Us?

MARK 1:21-28

I want to start tonight with Flannery O'Connor. She wrote a remarkable little story called "Revelation." The story is set in a doctor's office waiting room in a small southern town about 60 years ago. A plump woman comes in with her husband and does what everybody does in waiting rooms: sizes up everybody else there.

You do this in waiting rooms, don't you? Or airports, or your English class, or at Cracker Barrel? (Fraternity rush is too obvious to mention.) You judge others, evaluate who and what they are and how you relate to them by what they're wearing or how they talk or what they look like.

In the story, the woman, Mrs. Turpin, enters the room and classifies everyone: a well-dressed, pleasant lady; a fat, ugly girl of 18 or 19, who reads and scowls; a child and grandmother who were "vacant and white trashy"; and a red-headed girl who was "not white-trash, just common." In this way, O'Connor tells us, "Mrs. Turpin occupied herself at night naming classes of people."

Mrs. Turpin carries on a pleasant conversation with the pleasant lady, establishing herself in the class pecking order and distancing herself from the white trash and the black delivery boy.

She is so grateful that Jesus had made her who she was—a good woman:

> If Jesus had said, "You can be high society and have all the money you want and be thin and svelte-like, but can't be a good woman with it," she would have had to say, "Well don't make me that then. Make me a good woman and it don't matter what else, how fat or how ugly or how poor!" Her heart rose. He had not made her a n—— or white-trash or ugly! He had made her herself and given her a little of everything. Jesus, thank you! she said.

Mrs. Turpin sounds much like the Pharisee in Jesus' story of the Pharisee and the Tax Collector. Two men go up to the Temple. The self-righteous one strides right up the front, bellows out his list of accomplishments, and loudly thanks God that he is not like the other fellow. The tax collector, a morally compromised character, averts his eyes and mutters, "God, be merciful to me, a sinner!" You can probably guess which one Jesus, the friend of sinners, says went home justified.

Jesus told this story, the Bible says, "to some who trusted in themselves that they were righteous." Well, Mrs. Turpin's self-righteousness is about to be attacked. While Mrs. Turpin is in mid-prattle, the fat, ugly girl of 18 or 19 with a scowling expression catapults her book at Mrs. Turpin, launches out of her seat and sinks her hands like clamps into the fleshy neck of the self-satisfied woman who was thanking Jesus moments before.

But the attack on Mrs. Turpin's self-righteousness isn't complete. As the girl is being restrained, she focuses eerily on Mrs. Turpin:

> "What you got to say to me?" [Mrs. Turpin] asked hoarsely and held her breath, waiting, as for a revelation. The girl raised her head.
>
> Her gaze locked with Mrs. Turpin's. "Go back to hell where you came from, you old wart hog," she whispered. Her voice was low but clear. Her eyes burned for a moment as if she saw with pleasure that her message had struck its target.

Mrs. Turpin had to be attacked and insulted by an angry troubled girl in order to be shaken out of her airtight system of self-righteousness. The person that she was had to be destroyed if there would be any hope of new understanding, new life. In typical O'Connor wit and irony, God used an unlikely messenger to deliver his message.

I talked to a friend about this story at lunch last week, and he asked, "Why is it that we've got to be attacked for God to get our attention?" It's a good question. The answer, I think, shows up in our reading from Mark tonight.

Jesus is teaching in the synagogue. A man comes in with an unclean spirit. His life is so fractured that a demonic spirit speaks in and through him. He is the kind of man that makes you very nervous when he comes in the room. He sees Jesus and cries out, "What have you to do with us, Jesus of Nazareth? Have you come to destroy us? I know who you are, the Holy One of God." Jesus rebukes the unclean spirit and sends him out of the man. The people are amazed and astonished.

The unclean spirit recognizes two crucial things here. He recognizes who Jesus is—the Holy One of God. But more than that, he recognizes what Jesus does—he destroys all that stands in the way of God. In the Greek, the grammar of "have you come to destroy us" could also be read "you have come to destroy us."

Obviously, the unclean spirit is speaking on behalf of the demonic world: Satan and his legions will ultimately be destroyed by the cross, resurrection, and return of Jesus Christ. What is not so obvious is that the man with the unclean spirit is also speaking for the congregation gathered at the synagogue to hear Jesus' teaching. "Have you come to destroy us?" refers not just to demonic activity, but also to human resistance to God.

I think this is true because of the language Mark uses to describe people's response to Jesus. Jesus causes astonishment with his new teaching. Mark uses eight different words to describe fear, resistance, and alarm when people encounter Jesus. Jesus makes people nervous.

Or at least he makes people nervous who are attached, like Mrs. Turpin or the Pharisee, to their own systems of righteousness. He makes people nervous who are attached to living their own life in their own way under their own command.

And just think back to the waiting room question. Who doesn't have their own system of self-righteousness in place? Who doesn't live at some level in his or her own way under his or her own command? "Have you come to destroy us?" I know that there is so much to be destroyed in me.

So my friend's question: why must God attack us to get our attention? It is because there is so much to be destroyed. Paul reminds us in Romans that we are God's enemies in the first place. Worse than "wart hogs." Enemies of God are to be destroyed. That is what the Law requires.

There is no way around it. In the first place, Jesus comes to disturb and then destroy. He comes to destroy any system of judgment or self-reliance that is in opposition to him. And it is painful.

I'd like to say very clearly how God works. The evidence is in our text tonight, not to mention all over the Bible. God destroys in love. And the fact that it is love makes it no less painful. But God raises to life that which he's destroyed. And the new life is joyful.

I got an email from someone the other day who understands this. He said, "I'm writing because everything in my life is going to hell, so the Lord must be working." This guy understands that Jesus destroys before he creates. God is the "Joy that seekest me through pain."

Remember Eustace, from Narnia, whose greed and selfishness turn him into a dragon? I've used the story from C. S. Lewis before, but it's so powerful and apt. Once a dragon, he does feel sorry and wish to be a boy again. He scratches off his scales but finds that the scales are on layer after layer after layer. He is helpless and in despair. Then Aslan the Lion arrives to peel off Eustace's scales with his sharp claws:

> The very first tear he made was so deep that I thought it had gone right into my heart. And when he began pulling the skin off, it hurt worse than anything I've ever felt. The only thing that made me able to bear it was just the pleasure of feeling the stuff peel off.

Where is this happening in your life right now? Probably the place of deepest pain, real pain. Who likes being called a wart hog from hell? Who likes being attacked? Who likes pain and death? Who wants their life to go to hell? Nobody. I wish it didn't have to be that way. But that is God's way. And really, it must be so. You can't put new wine into old wineskins. The old has gone and the new is come. The old Adam dies, the new creation is raised. You just can't fix the old. God must make something new.

I was with a couple from another parish recently whose marriage had gone to hell. The woman was in the deepest despair she'd ever felt. Both husband and wife are believing Christians. Yet the pain was unbearable. They spent the day crying together. They prayed together. They mourned together for the ways they hadn't loved each other. The woman described the day as a funeral.

Then an amazing thing happened. The woman had had chronic back problems for years. At the end of the day that was a funeral for their marriage, her back was healed. Then the Lord opened up the channels of communication between the husband and wife. Hope flooded in. Joy came in the morning. The patterns of their married life that were opposed to God's desires were destroyed so that he could raise up a new life for them! And he did.

So too with Mrs. Turpin. At the end of the story, she has another "revelation." She has a vision of a throng of people: black, white, trashy, landowners, all mixed up together being taken up into heaven. Her judgments and conceptions are destroyed. Then she's given new life.

After Aslan rips off his scales, Eustace is thrown into a pool. Then he finds he's a boy again, a *new* boy.

Jesus did command the unclean spirit to come out of the man. The spirit convulsed the man and then fled. And the man was given a new life.

God destroys. But he destroys in love so that he can raise something new. This is the pattern of our life because that was his life. He was destroyed. Jesus who came to destroy was destroyed himself. He experienced real pain, real death, real hopelessness, real forsakenness utterly. On the cross he was utterly destroyed. And then he was raised.

God destroys and then he raises to life. Where you are being destroyed is where you are being raised. Sorrow lasts for the night, but joy does come in the morning.

Amen.

February 23, 2014 ‡ *Seventh Sunday after Epiphany (A)*

What Does the Fox Say?

MATTHEW 5:38-48

I think we can safely file our Gospel reading this morning under that famous quote: "It ain't those parts of the Bible that I can't understand that bother me—it's the parts that I do understand."

Jesus' exacting demand is all too easy to understand: "Do not resist an evildoer. But if anyone strikes you on the right cheek, turn the other also; and if anyone wants to sue you and take your coat, give your cloak as well; and if anyone forces you to go one mile, go also the second mile. Give to everyone who begs from you, and do not refuse anyone who wants to borrow from you." All this is summed up in the command, "Love your enemies."

There is no 'nuance' in what Jesus says here. There is no room for *just war theory, or what about Hitler, or what are you supposed to do when someone threatens someone you love, or you shouldn't give money to beggars because they will use it for alcohol and anyway it reinforces dependence.* And what about justice? Don't we need to do everything we can to stop oppression and evil?

Before we get 'up in arms,' to use a deliberately martial phrase, I'm not saying that all these issues aren't normal or valid concerns. And this is not a sermon about pacifism or the right role of military intervention. I hope this is a sermon that tries to take Jesus' words seriously and at face value. And more than that, how can "love your enemies" be a word of hope for us in our everyday lives?

The 17th-century Anglican dissenter George Fox seemed to take Jesus' words at face value. Though he himself was beaten and imprisoned for his preaching, he said:

> Ye are called to peace, therefore follow it; and that peace is in Christ, not in Adam in the fall. All that pretend to fight for Christ are deceived; for his kingdom is not of this world, therefore his servants do not fight. Fighters are not of Christ's kingdom, but are without Christ's kingdom; his kingdom stands in peace and righteousness, ... who came to save men's lives. ... all that talk of fighting for Sion are in darkness; for Sion needs no such helpers.

And yet just about anyone's normal and natural reaction is to do the opposite of what Jesus says this morning. If Fox is right, we may all be without Christ's kingdom, in thought if not in deed. We resist an evildoer, often in the name of Christ and his kingdom. And if someone hits us in the face, literally or metaphorically, we either hit back or want to hit back. Most of us certainly aren't praying in that moment for our enemies.

The *strike-back-and-defend-yourself* instinct seems to be written into our DNA. In the Old South, what Jesus expressly condemns was called "defending one's honor." A book called *Rot, Riot, and Rebellion* describes the early years of the University of Virginia. As you might gather from the title, things did not start off well. Mr. Jefferson had hoped that the young scholars would not need any outside discipline, that the love of learning and the goodness of their hearts would make for a peaceful, "academical" community, with professors and students living and learning together on the Lawn.

Unfortunately, Mr. Jefferson's hopes for UVA, while noble, were also naïve. He died shortly after the University's beginning, but not before many incidents of violence and what his enemies called "vicious irregularities." Drunkenness, gun duels, knife fights, visiting prostitutes, and gambling were par for the course on Grounds, or as UVA's initial enemies described its location, a "poor, old turned-out field." Bricks were thrown through professors' windows and their families terrorized. It was even reported that in November 1832, "a gang of drunken students interrupted divine services at a Charlottesville church"—that would be us!—"by standing outside of it and singing corn songs." ("Corn songs" were songs about sex!)

One raucous riot brought the ailing Jefferson down from Monticello to address the students. He was so overcome with grief at their behavior that he just broke down in tears. He was finally moved to deliver an angry harangue when he discovered that one of the chief perpetrators of the riot was his own grandson!

In an attempt to create order, Mr. Jefferson appealed to the young gentlemen's sense of honor. But their sense of honor was really the root cause of much of the mayhem. If one was slighted in any way, shape, or form, then one had to retaliate in order to retain one's honor. If you were "dissed," as we might have said a few years ago, then you had to fight back to protect your honor. Turning the other cheek, as Jesus suggests in the Gospel, was clearly not an option.

Mr. Jefferson was onto something good when appealing to some kind of inside motivation to affect change. The Board, when faced with the students' desultory display, imposed draconian restrictions. Mandatory wake-up call was 5 a.m. Students had to be in uniform. Local taverns were fined if they served students. And yet none of these laws helped; they only made things worse. We'll see in a moment that it would take something very different to save the University.

But think about your life for a moment. How has your honor been offended and you feel like fighting back? Or you have already fought back, which caused your enemy to fight back again and kept the whole cycle going. Where does it end? I was thinking, we all know that an eye for an eye leaves the whole world blind, but I guess that also means that a tooth for a tooth means nobody will be able to chew their steak or eat an apple. As a man with some tooth problems, the second part of the saying worries me!

On the one hand it sounds like Jesus is being as impractical as you could possibly be when he says to turn the other cheek. And yet, isn't what he says the most practical response possible? Here's a sound bite takeaway from the sermon in the same vein as the Gospel reading: *never defend yourself.* If you want to stop an argument, then just don't defend yourself. Period. Not a mumblin' word.

I heard of one minister who took this tack. When criticized or attacked, he would respond to himself, "If they only knew what terrible things were really in my heart, then they would say much worse." Never defend yourself. And you sure don't need to defend God, because—what does (the) Fox say?—Sion needs no such helpers. Walt Whitman thought so too. He said, "George Fox stands for ... the deepest, most eternal thought latent in the human soul. This is the thought of God, merged in the thoughts of moral right and the immortality of identity. Great, great is this thought—aye, greater than all else."

Passive, non-reaction is the only thing that will really break a cycle of violence and destruction. Except when it doesn't, because sometimes non-resistance may lead to death. Jesus gave no guarantees about that, other than saying, "Do not fear those who kill the body but cannot kill the soul."

Sometimes it does take a death to really change things. That is exactly what happened at the University, on November 12, 1840. Around 9 p.m., Law Professor John Davis (a member of our Christ Church vestry back then) stepped out of his pavilion to try to quiet the latest riot. He saw a masked student hiding behind one of his pillars: "Davis jumped for him and reached to unmask the small, bothersome student. The student fled but turned after a few steps, pointed his pistol, and without uttering a word, fired at Davis's gut."

Davis died two days later. Students were horrified and ashamed. Davis' death didn't completely end the rot, riot, and rebellion, but it marked a major turning point in the atmosphere of the University. As a result of his death, the honor system as we know it emerged—not defending your honor against insult with violence, but pledging honorable academic behavior.

Sometimes it does take a death to really change things. Well, you know where we're going and where we'll end. The One who said these words also lived these words and died these words. He didn't defend himself. He didn't say a mumblin' word. He told Peter to put down his sword when Peter raised it in defense, because those who take up the sword will perish by the sword.

And he was put to death, without anyone to defend him, without anyone to help him. He died to bring you and me from outside his kingdom into his kingdom. The Bible calls us "enemies of God," yet he loved his enemies.

His death changed everything, because on the third day he was raised, with nobody's help—nobody's but God's, that is. Because Sion needs no such helpers.

Amen.

February 27, 2011 ‡ *Eighth Sunday after Epiphany (A)*

Start Acting Like a Baby!

MATTHEW 6:24-34

In Washington, DC, at a Metro station, on a cold January morning in 2007, a man with a violin played six Bach pieces for about 45 minutes. During that time, approximately 2,000 people went through the station, most of them on their ways to work. After about three minutes, a middle-aged man noticed that a musician was playing. He slowed his pace and stopped for a few seconds, and then he hurried on to meet his schedule.

About four minutes later, the violinist received his first dollar. A woman threw money in the hat and, without stopping, continued to walk.

A young man leaned against the wall to listen to him, then looked at his watch and started to walk again.

After 10 minutes, a 3-year-old boy stopped, but his mother tugged him along hurriedly. The child stopped to look at the violinist again, but the mother pulled hard and the child continued to walk, turning his head the whole time. Several other children slowed down to listen, but every parent—without exception—forced their children to move on quickly. The musician played continuously. Only six people stopped and listened for a short while. About 20 gave money but continued to walk at their normal pace.

The man collected a total of 32 dollars. When the man with the violin finished playing, silence took over. No one noticed. No one applauded. There was no recognition at all.

What is interesting about this episode? The violinist was Joshua Bell, one of the greatest musicians in the world. He played one of the most intricate pieces ever written, with a violin worth 3.5 million dollars. Two days earlier, Joshua Bell played to a sold-out theater in Boston. The seats averaged 100 dollars each. He played the same music as he did in the hustle of the Metro.

What are we to make of this social experiment organized by the *Washington Post*? We might say that you shouldn't expect anyone to stop and smell the roses, or listen to the music on a busy morning when there are trains to catch, deadlines to meet, and bills to pay. The parents of those children might love to stop and listen to Bach, but then they would be late for their department meeting. And if they are late for their department meeting, then they might put their job in jeopardy. And if they put their job in jeopardy, then they might put their livelihood in jeopardy. And if they put their livelihood in jeopardy, then they might put their children in jeopardy.

OK, all that might be true, but I'm going to ask you for a minute to suspend your disbelief—to stop thinking about this episode like a grown-up and to start thinking about it from the vantage point of one of the children. They didn't know that Joshua Bell was supposed to be brilliant. Nor did they suspect the musician was a homeless panhandler who should have put down his violin and picked up the classifieds. They were just mesmerized by the music. Imagine the situation from their perspective. After all, Jesus did say "whoever does not receive the kingdom of God as a little child will never enter it."

I think it is with those same childlike ears that we are to hear what Jesus says in today's Gospel: "do not worry about your life, what you will eat or what you will drink, or about your body, what you will wear. ... do not worry about tomorrow."

I was talking with a college student about this passage this week. He, like most of us, tends to worry about his life—not so much about what he will eat or what he will wear, but what he will do when he graduates from college. But then you talk to people in their early to mid 20s, and they have the same worries about their lives—whom they will marry, if they will marry, where they will live, what kind of vocation they will have. And then, of course, the same issues affect us all the way through our lives.

The fun never ends: you start worrying about your children or your health. I was sick two weeks ago for several days, so I did what any responsible person does when he's ill: I looked up my symptoms on WebMD. I was convinced that I was a goner. If you don't worry about your health, you worry about your finances, your grandchildren, and your retirement. Rare is the person who does not worry about tomorrow. Rare is the person who stops in the Metro and listens to Bach.

This student talked about his father reading him this verse ever since he was young. If he was stressed about school his father would assure him. "Look at the birds of the air; they neither sow nor reap nor gather into barns, and yet your heavenly Father feeds them." If he was worried about relationships, his father would him remind him, "And can any of you by worrying add a single hour to your span of life?" What a good dad.

Jesus is clearly saying that when you are worrying you are not trusting. And Jesus is clearly saying that God loves you and God will provide for you. God is trustworthy. To believe in God is not really a set of objective intellectual assertions that you must sign on to. The way the Bible talks about belief is more in line with trust. To believe is to trust your Heavenly Father the way a little child, a toddler, an infant even, trusts her parents.

In fact, the Greek word for "child" that Jesus uses when he tells us how we must accept the kingdom is better translated "nursing infant." I love all the babies that we have at Christ Church now. There is no better picture of trust and dependency than a nursing infant. I hereby declare all babies under 12 months to be our spiritual leaders! We should start having vestry meetings in the nursery. Don't stop acting like a baby; start acting like one!

Trusting in the God who provides for you is the antidote for worrying about your tomorrow. Obviously, I'm not telling you anything you don't already know. Like my friend's father, I am reminding you of what you already know to be true about God. The problem is this: the journey from your head to your heart is the longest journey in the world. What you know to be true sometimes doesn't help you when your tomorrow looks iffy and your today isn't looking so hot either. And in the day to day, it is so easy to forget about "seek[ing] first for the kingdom of God," as Jesus says in the passage, which is just another way to say trusting God. Seeking is trusting.

Instead, most of us are like the man in the well-worn preacher joke. The man falls off a cliff and grabs a branch jutting out from the rock face. As he dangles hundreds of feet in the air he calls out to God. "God, if you are there, *help me!*" To his surprise, he hears a voice from heaven saying, "I'm here, my son. Just let go and I will catch you. Trust me." The man pauses a few seconds and calls out, "Is there anyone else up there?" As Jesus says in the passage, we are the "you of little faith."

An Episcopal minister named William Porcher DuBose perfectly articulates the distance between head knowledge and heart reality when it comes to trusting God. He also gives us some insight into what it means to seek first the kingdom of God, to trust God like a nursing infant. Dubose graduated from UVA in 1859 and was ordained and worked as a chaplain during the Civil War. Afterwards he taught theology at Sewanee.

In a letter to his wife during the war, a time when he had every reason to "worry about his life," Dubose wrote,

> How is it that we will so often stray away from God when it is so sweet to be near Him and so full of discomfort and wretchedness to be far from Him? If our hope rested on our own faithfulness how miserable we'd be! But blessed be God, it rests upon His faithfulness and not ours.

My experience is that I will not willingly trust God until I see how miserable I am without him. I will try every other avenue until all the avenues lead to dead ends, full of discomforts. Then, when I just can't hold on to the branch any longer, I will let go, but not of my own volition. I will just fall because my grip fails. And every time, God is there. Oh, me of little faith. It's a good thing my hope rests on his faithfulness and not mine.

Somerset Maugham's novel *The Razor's Edge* is a brilliant exposé of where people put their trust for their lives. One character lives for social respectability, seeing and being seen by all the right people. He dies as an old man, cursing a woman who did not invite him to the event of the social season. Another couple lives for money. They are ruined by the crash of 1929. Another man lives for art. He remains ironic and distant. And finally, the hero seeks spiritual enlightenment from all the sources of wisdom throughout the ages. In a very real way, he is trying to "seek first the kingdom of God." He ends his journey by spending years at the foot of a guru in India, attaining peace through austere self-abnegation.

Yet in the end, even the spiritually enlightened hero has lived a life of trust in the self. He is no better off than the socialite who demands to be buried in his aristocratic ancestor's costume. If our hope rests on our own faithfulness, how miserable we are.

The Gospel announcement is that we do not have to go seeking anywhere for God. As DuBose says, "God has placed forever before our eyes, not the image but the very Person of the Spiritual Man. We have not to ascend into Heaven to bring Him down, nor to descend into the abyss to bring Him up, for He is with us, and near us, and in us." As you go through the Metro station of your life, so anxious about your planes, trains, and automobiles, God is there with you, near you, in you. His song is a beautiful song: "Therefore I tell you, do not worry about your life." It is a song that will always and forever turn the heads of children.

Amen.

March 9, 2011 ‡ *Ash Wednesday*

The End of Scorekeeping

MATTHEW 6:1-6

I took my son to see the Harlem Globetrotters last Sunday. As I'm sure you know, the Globetrotter shows are a mix of dazzling athletic ability and outrageous slapstick humor. The Globetrotters always play the Washington Generals. But mostly they just play with each other and play with the referees and play with the kids in the crowd.

Like any basketball game, it features a scoreboard and an announcer who periodically announces the score. But no one really pays attention to the score. Of course, the Globetrotters almost always beat the Generals, but nobody really cares about the score, especially the Globetrotters. They are too busy having fun and making sure that the crowd is having fun, too.

Can you imagine a life lived without the tyranny of a scoreboard? Most of us keep score all the time, in every imaginable arena. Marriages are so often reduced to scorekeeping: *I did this for you, and you've done nothing for me. I changed the baby's last two diapers, while you slept a full 8 hours.* Friendships are full of scorekeeping too: *I've called you the last five times, but you only call me when you when it fits into your agenda.* Sibling relationships are chock full of scorekeeping: *I've been the one to take care of Dad since he got sick, while you're living it up in California.*

You keep score at school or at work, too—your grades or your titles, your paychecks or your promotions. You even do it in your own body, with the scales or with the number of runs you've gotten in this week.

The Gospel passage for this Ash Wednesday is about scorekeeping with God. It's a way that God and everyone else will know that you are winning the game of religion. To this Jesus says, "Beware of practicing your piety before others in order to be seen by them." Jesus says, when you give money or pray or fast, do so in such a way that nobody knows what you are doing. When he says nobody, he means *nobody*, including yourself: "Do not let your left hand know what your right hand is doing." Jesus says you can't even keep your own score.

The theological name for scorekeeping is "justification by works." It's a way of living life as if it were a contest to be won, a battle out of which one must emerge the victor, an accusation against which one must justify oneself. This is the way of the old Adam, and frankly put, it is the way of death. Justification by works is a closed circle. You can never justify yourself enough; you must always keep striving.

The *Onion*, with its usual piercing insight into the human condition, spoofed the idea behind scorekeeping and justification by works in a recent article about music star Kanye West:

Following the widespread acclaim and media adulation over his latest album, *My Beautiful Dark Twisted Fantasy*, multimillion-selling recording artist Kanye West announced Wednesday that he had finally received the exact amount of approval he needed to attain and had therefore retired from the entertainment industry to live on a small farm in Iowa.

Though known for his outsized ego and grandstanding lyrics, West said "all of that is over now," telling reporters outside his remote two-bedroom farmhouse that after years of nonstop public attention, he was now completely secure in his sense of self and required no further affirmation.

"My goal all along was to be praised and talked about until I reached a level of total contentment with who I am and where I belong in the world, and on Friday night of last week, I reached that level," said West, standing outside the screen door of his home in a pair of khaki slacks and a plain gray work shirt. "I finally feel satisfied and whole as a human being, which means I can stop being a famous pop star now."

Like the *Onion*, Ash Wednesday strips the self-justifying emperor of all of his ridiculous and petty clothes. In the words of a brilliant essay by one of our parishioners, Ash Wednesday reminds us "of the core truth of Christianity: we must give up. We must give up not this or that habit or food or particular sin, but the entire project of self-justification, of making God's love contingent on our own achievements."

The writer goes on:

> We are reminded, both by the words we say and the burned palms imposed on our foreheads, that we will die. Ashes to ashes, dust to dust. Give up! Give up, for you will not escape death. The entire logic of the theology of glory, of all our Pelagian impulses, of all human attempts at mastery and control, are searched out and stripped away on Ash Wednesday. We are seen for what we are—frail mortals. All power, all money, all self-control, all striving, all efforts at reform cannot permanently forestall our death. Our return to dust is the looming fact of our existence that, in our resistance to it, provides a template of sorts for all the more petty efforts we make to gain control of our lives.

The message of Ash Wednesday is that though your death and my death make a mockery of the scoreboard, there was and is another's death that renders all scorekeeping in life utterly absurd. For Jesus' death on the cross has once and for all justified you.

There is no more to be done. There is just life to be lived. There are referees to be teased, children to be played with, men and women to be loved. Though we may wish to continue to let our left hand and everyone else know what our right hand is doing, the truth of the matter is that God is not keeping score.

Amen.

February 20, 2015 ‡ *Friday before the First Sunday of Lent (B)*

The Cathedral Church of the Advent in Birmingham, Alabama

The Crack Is How the Light Gets In

MARK 1:9-15

The lectionary reading for this upcoming Sunday, the first Sunday of Lent, is Mark's account of Jesus' baptism in the Jordan River. We do a lot of baptisms at Christ Church, and I'm sure there are lots here at the Advent, too. Every baptism is a special and wonderful event.

Yet none that I've done so far have had the audiovisual fanfare that accompanied Jesus' baptism. As Jesus is baptized by his cousin John, the heavens are torn apart, the Holy Spirit descends on him in the form of a dove, and God says, "You are my Son, the Beloved; with you I am well pleased."

Pretty dramatic, but, in fact, there is no indication in Mark that anyone else other than Jesus actually hears or sees anything. It is as though God the Father is speaking intimately and directly to his Son. He is preparing him for all that is to come.

Mark uses the interesting word, "torn apart." The heavens were "torn apart," rather than "opened" as in Matthew and Luke. The Greek word there is a form of the verb schizo, as in schism or schizophrenia. It is not the same word as "opened." You open the door. You close the door. The door looks the same, but something torn apart is not easily closed again. Tear apart the fabric of a shirt or glossy print of a photograph. The ragged edges never go back together as they were.

The handle of my favorite coffee mug broke off in the dishwasher the other day. It was a gift from my daughter when she was little; she had painted and glazed it. The break was fairly clean, so I got some Gorilla Glue and put it back together. A tiny piece was still missing, and I was worried that it would collapse again and I'd spill hot coffee all over my lap. I took the risk because I want the ragged edges to go back together as they were. But they never do.

You have experienced, and perhaps are now experiencing, some kind of tearing apart in your life. It's February, and you may notice that there are always a lot of deaths in the cold of winter. The obit pages are always full this time of year. Someone's absence means that the edges of family life can never go back together as they were.

Of course, it doesn't take anything as traumatic as death to tear apart a life. Even happy events, like a child graduating or getting married tear apart how things are. There is always some kind of tearing apart that is happening; entropy is always at work in life. Mugs break. People leave. Life changes. Edges no longer fit together as they once did. In fact, two weeks after I glued the handle back on the mug, it broke with a full cup of coffee in it, spilling all over the bedroom floor.

The good news is that the torn open places are not all bad news. In fact, the torn open place in the heavens at Jesus' baptism was where God came in. The Spirit descended like a dove through the torn open place. God spoke his words of loving assurance—"You are my Son, the Beloved; with you I am well pleased"—through the torn open place. The fact that everything won't be the same can be a very good thing. God is in the torn open places.

Leonard Cohen sings about this in his song called "Anthem." He sings,

> Ring the bells that still can ring.
> Forget your perfect offering.
> There is a crack, a crack in everything.
> That's how the light gets in.

God's light shines through the cracks that are in you and me. Yes, our lives are cracked. Yes, everything is cracked. And yes, that is how the light gets in.

The movie *Wild* was released at the end of last year. It's based on a book by Cheryl Strayed, who tells the story of her life being torn open when her mother dies of cancer at 45 years old. Cheryl is in her early 20s. At first, through the enormous crack in her life comes not light but chaos and darkness. In order to numb her pain, she turns to sex, random hook-up after random hook-up, even though she is married to a faithful husband. She also starts using heroin, telling her counselor that sex and heroin were the only things that made her feel any better about the torn-open place in her life.

Strayed decides to hike the Pacific Coast Trail in order to deal with her pain. Although she's an inexperienced hiker, she makes the 1,100-mile journey alone. Although there is no positive mention of God, the book and movie are not as self-helpy as one might expect. In fact, at the end of her hike, having delved deeply into her grief, having lived inside the torn-open place, she asks,

> What if I forgave myself? I thought. What if I forgave myself even though I'd done something I shouldn't have? What if I was a liar and a cheat and there was no excuse for what I'd done other than because it was what I wanted and needed to do? What if I was sorry, but if I could go back in time I wouldn't do anything differently than I had done? ... What if what made me do all those things everyone thought I shouldn't have done was what also had got me here? What if I was never redeemed? What if I already was?

I suspect that Strayed may be underestimating the cost of her destructive response to her pain—the cost on herself, her ex-husband, and others around her. But I do think she's onto something. God does use all things to work together for good. St. Paul tells us this in the eighth chapter of Romans. What's more, the crack in all things, the torn-openness of all things, is the doorway of his light. And she's right in asking her final question—*What if I already was redeemed?*

The great hope and comfort of the Gospel is that we already are redeemed. We know this because of another tearing apart. It happened three years after the heavens were torn apart and Jesus came up dripping out of the baptismal waters, hearing a voice saying, "You are my Son." This time he hung on a cross, his hands and feet and brow torn apart by nails and thorns.

Scripture tells us that as Jesus was crucified for us, the curtain of the temple was torn apart. This was the barrier between heaven and earth, between God and humanity. Up till now, only the high priest could go behind that veil into the Holy of Holies, into God's presence.

But when Jesus died, scripture says, "At that moment the curtain of the temple was torn in two, from top to bottom. The earth shook, and the rocks were split." As one preacher put it, this time in the tearing apart,

> there was no voice from the darkened heavens that day. God was silent, not even a whisper.
>
> But there was a voice not far off but close. Not up but down. A centurion soldier stood at the foot of the cross keeping order, marking time, waiting to pronounce death. When he saw that Jesus had breathed his last, he said, "Truly this man was God's Son."

The curtain was torn apart so that you and I could enter into the loving, healing, redeeming presence of God. And never again will that curtain fit together as it once did. It is through the crack in the curtain that God's light gets in. It will never, ever stop shining, no matter what in your life is torn apart. That is because you are already redeemed.

Amen.

March 5, 2017 ‡ *First Sunday in Lent (A)*

Considering the Great Weight

ROMANS 5:12-19

I'll begin with a humorous anecdote because even though this is the beginning of Lent and this sermon is heavy on sin, that doesn't mean we can't find some humor in the whole situation. And don't worry—a sermon heavy on sin is also commensurately heavy on grace.

My friend Drew Rollins is the Episcopal chaplain at Louisiana State University in Baton Rouge. He sent me an article about a foreign exchange student from Greece who got his car towed from an LSU parking lot and was fined $250 for parking in a restricted area. The sign in the restricted area said, "Greeks Only." The young man apparently did not realize "Greeks Only" meant members of the fraternity and sorority community. He challenged the fine, saying, "I am Greek, the sign says Greek, and so I parked here. I do not understand the problem. ... I do not want trouble, I just came here for an American experience. I would like to go to a school baseball game and meet American girls at Mardi Gras; not to fight with anyone."

Sometimes even when you think you're right, you're still in trouble and there is still a fine to pay. This funny scene helps us understand the way St. Paul talks about sin in today's reading from Romans. We tend to think of sin as discrete acts—individual and separate behaviors that are, well, indiscreet—imprudent, injurious, thoughtless. I shouldn't have eaten that extra piece of cake, shouldn't have said that terrible thing about my co-worker, shouldn't have gotten drunk and hooked up, shouldn't have embezzled the company funds, shouldn't have been trading in child-pornography.

It's true that all those discrete actions I mentioned (minus, maybe, the extra piece of cake) are injurious and accurately described as sinful. You may have even noticed an ascending order of injuriousness in my list, at least as most people appraise sinful acts.

Although not everyone agrees on what is sinful. A recent survey by the Barna Group discovered that the top three sins according to most Americans are 1) procrastination 2) overeating (I guess we need to put the extra piece of cake back in the list, after all), and 3) spending too much time consuming media. I'm guessing you can pretty easily do all three at once: eat a pint of Cherry Garcia ice cream while binge watching Game of Thrones instead of doing your taxes. You've just committed the trifecta of modern sins in one fell-swoop, and you didn't even have to leave your couch.

The point is that all of this has only the most tenuous connection to what St. Paul means when he uses the word "sin." Paul says, "sin came into the world through one man, and death came through sin, and so death spread to all because all have sinned." Paul is referencing the story in Genesis where Adam and Eve, our first parents and the representatives of all human beings, rebelled against God and chose their own way above his. As Paul says, "one man's trespass led to condemnation for all." As a result of that "vast primordial catastrophe," as Cardinal Newman describes it, death was ushered into the world.

We don't like to face up to this truth, but deep down, we suspect there is, or at least might be, a problem. Like David Byrne sings in the Talking Heads' song "Psycho Killer," "I can't seem to face up to the facts. / I'm tense and nervous and I can't relax." So we come up with systems to justify ourselves in the face of this condemnation: *I'm not so bad. He is worse. It's not my fault. Don't lump me in with Adam and Eve. Nobody's perfect. This offends my sense of self-esteem.*

Two of our favorite theologians—Calvin and Hobbes—illustrate this point. I'm talking about the little boy and his tiger. In this comic, it's close to Christmas, and Calvin is worried about getting presents from Santa.

> Calvin: I'm getting nervous about Christmas.
> Hobbes: You're worried you haven't been good?
> Calvin: That's just the question. It's all relative. What's Santa's definition? How good do you have to be to qualify as good? I haven't *killed* anybody. ... I haven't committed any felonies. I didn't start any wars. ... Wouldn't you say that's pretty good? Wouldn't you say I should get lots of presents?
> Hobbes: But maybe good is more than the absence of bad.
> Calvin: See, *that's* what worries me.

Sin, in St. Paul's view, is so much more than a list of wrongdoings. Sin is not just individual peccadilloes but a corporate, inexorable, and overwhelming Power. It is a disastrous and malign force that holds us hostage until we are manipulated into its endgame, namely Death. Sin is to be catastrophically separated from God's goodness and endlessly trapped within your worst self. No one escapes its malevolent and ultimately fatal reach—the fraternity of Adam is the most comprehensive community of all. It is universal. As Paul says, "all die in Adam."

Our predicament is much, much worse than we thought. Maybe it would be better to have the extra piece of cake after all. Under the power and dominion of Sin, we are like our young friend from Greece: even when we think we're safe and okay, we are in big, big trouble. Even when we think we are opening the right envelope, we are opening the wrong envelope. And the fine we owe is much, much more than $250. Our very lives are demanded of us by the Powers of Sin and Death.

Our response to the Power of Sin grossly underestimates this Power. We think we can just "make good choices" and everything will be okay. If we just get ourselves together spiritually, we won't get towed away. But this is because, like the medieval theologian St. Anselm said, "we have not yet considered the great weight of sin." As I said, this sermon is heavy on sin because sin is *ponderous*— from the Latin *pondus*, a great burdensome weight.

Drew Rollins illustrated this with a really funny story at our parish retreat. I'll use his words:

> Jeanie and I both very clearly remember having one of my younger cousins visit us in New Orleans. I didn't know him very well. But he came through town and stopped in for a quick visit. At this stage, we had David and John (maybe around 4 and 2 years of age). When Cousin Thayer arrived for dinner, the house was its usual total chaos. Jeanie was trying to get the kids ready for bed, pick up the house, fix dinner, converse with this cousin.
>
> Thayer was maybe 26, a young banker. He showed up in a blue suit looking very put together. He and his wife were about to have their first child. With this chaotic scene unfolding in front of us, I commented knowingly to him, "Well, I guess you guys are getting ready for a pretty big change in your lives, aren't you?" And he responded *with great confidence*, "Well, we don't think it's going to be much of a change for us. We're both *very organized*." Jeanie and I just looked at each other. You can't explain to that young man that he will not be able to *organize* himself out of the problem that he is about to face!

No matter how hard we try, how disciplined we are, how virtuous we are, we cannot organize our way out of the Power of Sin. We are all complicit in the disobedience of Adam and Eve. As C. S. Lewis says, "fallen man is not simply an imperfect creature who needs improvement: he is a rebel who needs to lay down his arms." And even after we've buried our guns in the ground, we still need someone to come and rescue us.

So here comes the commensurate grace. St. Paul says, "For if the many died through the one man's trespass, much more surely have the grace of God and the free gift in the grace of the one man, Jesus Christ, abounded for the many. ... Therefore just as one man's trespass led to condemnation for all, so one man's act of righteousness leads to justification and life for all."

Simply put, your *only* hope is in the death and resurrection of Jesus Christ. Nothing else, nowhere else, no one else. Christianity is remarkably simple. It is ostentatiously straightforward. You are held captive to the Powers of Sin and Death and are entirely powerless to help yourself or anyone else. Jesus Christ alone is "mighty to save."

And save he did, when he took the great weight of sin on his crucified shoulders. And save he did, when he paid our fine with his blood. And save he did, when he ransomed us from death. And save he did, when the great weight of the stone sealing the tomb was rolled away like a pebble. And save he *does*, as he takes the weight from your shoulders and gives you in exchange the free gift of righteousness.

Amen.

January 21, 2007 ‡ *First Sunday in Lent (B)*

Where
the Wild
Things Are

MARK 1:9-13

T here is a classic children's book that I read growing up, and I bet you read it, too: *Where The Wild Things Are*, by Maurice Sendak. It's about a boy named Max who gets sent to his room for being too wild and then fantasizes about sailing to an island full of dark and wild and scary creatures.

It won the Caldecott Medal for most distinguished picture book of the year when it was published, but I just found it really scary. Like the flying monkeys in *The Wizard of Oz*, *Where the Wild Things Are* left me uneasy.

In our passage from Mark this evening, Jesus gets sent to where the wild things are. After his baptism, the Spirit drives him into the wilderness, an uneasy place filled with the dark and the wild and the scary. Satan tempts him. And in a detail found only in Mark's account of this story, we see that Jesus is out among the wild animals. For 40 days and nights, Jesus is where the wild things are.

Mark's details are important. The Gospel is blunt, compact. His story displays "the three C's" of good writing: it is clear, concise, and cogent. Now, why the wild animals?

It would be nice to think of Jesus as Dr. Doolittle. We read elsewhere in Scripture that all things, including the wild animals, were created through him. So one supposes that Jesus could relate to the wild animals, even if only as a kind of horse whisperer. It would be nice to think that the animals helped him out there in the wilderness, tempted by Satan. Perhaps the lions and hyenas comforted Jesus as he fasted and suffered. We might think that Jesus is kind of PETA poster child, respecting the innate dignity of every venomous spider and bloodsucking bat.

But that's not at all what Mark has in mind. The setting is the wilderness—that is not a good thing. All through the Old Testament, blessing and peace are associated with inhabited and cultivated land. The wilderness is the place associated with the curse. As one commentator says about the wilderness, "Man cannot live there. Only frightening and unwanted kinds of animals dwell there. ... Jesus confronts the horror, the loneliness and the danger with which the wilderness is fraught when he meets the wild beasts."

Jesus is where the wild things are. Why?

The first thing to say is that Jesus is *with us* where the wild things are. As his life is a pattern for our lives, we know that our lives are marked by wilderness and temptation.

Does this come as a surprise? What's interesting is that as soon as Jesus is baptized, the Spirit drives him to the wilderness. There is a misconception out there promulgated by prosperity Gospel preachers that Christian life is trouble free, victorious, and easy. The juxtaposition of Jesus' baptism and his immediate experience of hunger, thirst, frightening creatures, unprotected nights, and fiendish temptation makes clear that Christian life is not all warm baths and comfort food. You may think, "With friends like God, who needs enemies." Nevertheless, to be a Christian is to be ushered at some point—at many points—into the wilderness.

Maybe you are in the wilderness right now in some part of your life. People who struggle with depression and anxiety understand wilderness. The hopelessness that is part of depression is cruel. When you are depressed, you feel as though you have no hope of getting better. When you are caught in anxiety, the minutes seem like years.

William Styron—he is one of my favorite writers; he died last month—suffered an episode of debilitating depression about 15 years ago and wrote a book about it called *Darkness Visible: A*

Memoir of Madness. "To most of those who have experienced it," Styron writes, "the horror of depression is so overwhelming as to be quite beyond expression."

You might wonder why I include anxiety and depression so often as examples in my sermons, and why my wife Christie regularly prays for people struggling in its grip. I'm a pastor. The battle against depression is so widespread in this and every congregation! I've experienced its ravages in a secondhand way through friends and family.

Toward the end of his ordeal, Styron concludes that "those who are suffering a siege ... [must] be told—be convinced, rather—that the illness will run its course." So to those tonight in the throes or even the edges of this anxious wilderness, please hear this: Jesus is with you. He is with you where the wild beasts are. Jesus is with you in the wilderness. Even though you may not believe it—and only the Holy Spirit can convince you—the passage from Mark shows that it's true: Jesus is with you where the wild things are.

Of course, wilderness takes on many forms: loneliness, insecurity, restlessness, relationship trauma. Maybe you've gone through a divorce, or your parents have. Maybe you've lost a child. For many in the world, the threat of the wild beast is actual and physical. Iraqis, Somalis, and Palestinians know this. As do the scores of mothers in American cities who have lost their sons to drugs and guns.

Others of us may not feel that we are in a wilderness period of life. But always present is temptation, even when (perhaps especially when) we are happy. Mark does not specify the devil's temptations in the way the other Gospels do, but we know that his temptation was severe. We also note that Mark doesn't record Jesus' victory over Satan here, nor the end of the temptation. This is because Satan sustained his temptation all throughout Jesus' life! The whole Gospel shows how Jesus was tempted.

There are so many temptations. You are already familiar with the more prosaic ones: sex, drugs, and rock 'n' roll. But I find the chief temptation of our Enemy to be this: just like he did to Eve in the Garden, he will whisper in your ear, "You could be like God." You are in control. You know what's best for your life. You need to manipulate and plan the future.

Those who have experienced both anxiety and the temptation to control the future will know that the two are intimately connected. We experience anxiety when we try to control the future—or others—because we are trying to do God's job.

Imagine showing up one morning and being expected to do the job of a nuclear physicist. Or if you happen to be a nuclear physicist, being asked to play center linebacker for the Chicago Bears. Who wouldn't be anxious? Similarly, the future is the Holy Spirit's job.

What have I said so far? Because of the immediate proximity of Jesus' baptism and his wilderness experience, we see that Christian life is filled with wilderness and temptation. I've also said—tried to convince you who are suffering—that Jesus is with you where the wild things are. He was there once, and he is there now, with you.

But we're not finished. Not only is Jesus *with you* in the wilderness, Jesus is *for you* in the wilderness. Those are the two words of Christian theology: God is with you, and God is for you. Ultimately, the truth that God is for you is the most powerful.

God is for you. To see why that is so powerful, let's take a step back. God, in the first place, is *against* you. Our deepest problem is God himself and his judgment on our innate sin. This is why, after having tried to usurp God's position, Eve's husband Adam said, "I heard the sound of you in the garden, and I was afraid, because I was naked; and I hid myself." Adam had to leave the garden, and he went to the wilderness.

God's Law, his standard for perfection in our lives, a standard that is a voice inside us that never ceases, is so severe that all we can say when he comes near is what Peter told Jesus: "Go away from me, Lord, for I am a sinful man!"

God himself is our problem. His law, his demand, his holiness is our problem. Our sin, our disobedience, our primal urge to be in control—these are in constant conflict with God. He is our deepest problem. He is the wildest of the wild things.

Yet the Gospel irony is that our deepest problem is our only solution to our problem! Because he who should be against us is actually for us!

Jesus is for us in the wilderness. As we said earlier, the wilderness is not a place where man can live. It is a place of the curse. That is because in the Bible, the wilderness is associated with the judgment of God. No one can live under the judgment of God. Who can live with the judgment of a spouse? Of a boss? Of a roommate? No one! We need a way out.

Well, the wilderness is associated not only with the judgment of God, but also with what precedes it in the text: the waters of baptism.

Although Jesus himself was sinless, he so identified himself with us, he is so "for us," that he submitted to baptism, taking on himself the judgment of the One from whom Adam hid, and the One from whom we hide.

He went to the wilderness where no man can live. The waters of baptism and the 40 days in the wilderness prefigure the final result of his taking on the judgment of God for us. Jesus did not live. He died. He died on a cross. He died on a cross under the judgment of God.

As Adam was expelled out of the Garden, as Jesus was driven out into the wilderness, the man who so identified himself with sinners carried a cross outside of the city gates. He died there on that cross, under the judgment of God. That death was meant for you and me.

This is what it means that Jesus is for you in the wilderness. His absolute identification with you puts to death the old Adam in you so that his death is your death. And you are now free. You are now free to be a creature who trusts God for the future, who depends on God in the wilderness.

Jesus is *with you* in the wilderness. Jesus is *for you* in the wilderness. Because of this, life is not and will not always be wilderness. Here we have "no continuing city." But make no mistake: because he has taken away the judgment of God, you are destined for a place where the wild things are banished to the outer darkness. And God himself is not your problem but the eternal and everlasting light of your days.

Amen.

February 14, 2016 ‡ *First Sunday in Lent (C)*

The Devil Is in the If-Thens

LUKE 4:1-13

The first Sunday in Lent gives us an account of Jesus being tempted by the devil. After Jesus is baptized, he fasts for 40 days in the wilderness. He is tempted by the devil during this time, and we get a snapshot of their encounter when the 40 days are over. This year I noticed an obvious point about the interaction that I'd somehow missed before. The insight is less about the content and more about the overall structure of the conversation between Jesus and the devil. *How* they say what they have to say is as revealing as *what* they say.

Have you noticed that the devil speaks in full conditional sentences? A full conditional sentence contains two clauses: the first a dependent clause, expressing the condition, and the second a main clause, expressing the consequence. Wikipedia's example of such a sentence is "if it rains, then the picnic will be canceled." Another possibility: "if the Cavaliers run the table and beat the Tar Heels at home, then they will be ACC basketball regular season champions."

The devil, who is not playing a game, says, *If you* are the Son of God, *then* tell this stone to become bread. *If you* worship me, *then* all this power and glory will be yours. And again, *If you* are the Son of God, *then* jump off the pinnacle of the temple and land safely. You may have heard the saying "the devil is in the details." A better maxim is "the devil is in the if-thens."

By the way, don't get sidetracked by conceptions of the devil as all red and pitchforky. Jeff Tweedy sings, "When the devil came to me / He was not red / He was chrome." I think I know what he's getting at, and we definitely know that Scripture attests to the existence of a being, malign and misanthropic, hell-bent on marring human happiness.

But even if you can't wrap your mind around a force whose *raison d'être* is to "corrupt and destroy the creatures of God" as we say in the baptismal liturgy, you can at least acknowledge the grotesque fault line that runs through all people, places, and things. The stabbing death of the 13-year-old girl by the Virginia Tech student would be just a recent testimony to gaping disorder in the world. Life is not the way it should be.

But let's get back to the grammar of Beelzebub. What is behind the devil's if-then phraseology? C. S. Lewis, whose still germane *Screwtape Letters* reveals that he knows a thing or two about the devil's ways and wiles, says it this way in another work, *God in the Dock:*

> One begins by thinking that if only something external happened; if only after the war you could get a better job, if only you could get a new house or if only your mother-in-law or daughter-in-law was no longer living with you; if something like that happened, then things would really be better.

I hope this line of thinking is faulty; my mother-in-law is about to move in with us. But who doesn't know the power of this devilish temptation? What is it for you? Money, sex, and power are the usual suspects. I'm not immune to that triad, and a few years ago I preached a sermon saying that if we just had crown molding in our living room I would be a happy, fulfilled homeowner and person.

Well, wouldn't you know, we put crown molding in the living room. And gosh darn it, it looks really good! And it made me happy for a month or two. Now, if we could just figure out a way to put in a master bathroom adjoining our bedroom, I'd be really happy. Apparently, when our house was built in 1952, people didn't have master baths. They must not have been very happy people because it is abundantly clear to me that if I had a master bath, then I would be happy.

When I was in fourth grade, I wanted to be Reggie Jackson—"Mr. October," the New York Yankees slugger. If I could just be Reggie I would be OK. My older, smarter brother asked, "Paul, if you were Reggie Jackson, then who would Reggie Jackson be?" This stumped me. I answered, "Um, I guess he would be me." My brother replied, "Then how do you know you aren't already Reggie Jackson?" This confused me. In fact, I'm still confused. I very well may be Reggie Jackson.

What I'm saying is ridiculous, of course. I should say that there are some basics that a person does actually need in life: food and shelter and safety and love. Justice and meaning are important, too. But my point about the temptation text this morning is that the devil deals in conditionality.

Some of his more searing conditional sentences include *if you were lovable, then you would be loved, if you had worth, then you would show your worth, if you were a better parent, then your children would be happy and successful.* The list goes on and on and on and on. One of the Father of Lies' favorite go-to lines is "if God is real, then bad things would not happen to you or to the world."

If the grammar of Satan is conditional, then the grammar of God is declarative. Jesus responds to each of the devil's temptations with a declarative statement from Scripture. "It is written," he says three times over: we live on more than bread; we must worship only God; we don't put God to the test. To each of the devil's slippery slopes, Jesus answers back with a solid rock. The stolid durability of Jesus' responses puts the devils if-thens to flight, at least for the moment. The devil would return at "an opportune time." More on that later.

What does the contrast between the conditional and the declarative mean for you and me? Most of us, whether we know it or not, slink into church Sunday after Sunday in hopes that God will "do us a solid" as the saying goes. (That phrase was coined by *Seinfeld*, by the way, as Kramer asked Jerry to help him out.) Life is tenuous enough without having to walk the if-then tightrope to secure ourselves.

I can tell you what you need because I need it, too. You need a power, a love, a force that is beyond condition, beyond our deserving. Because you fail from time to time to do the ifs in life, you need someone to step between the first and second clauses of the full conditional sentence. You need someone to step between cause and effect, the condition and the consequence. You need someone solid enough to take the heat of your failure.

I love what Bono says in the song "God Part II." He recognizes the reality of the devil's temptations, and the way we fail to live up to how life should be, even how we think we should be. Where have you fallen in your own fault line? When you are lost in the conditionality of the devil's temptations, and falling into your own fault line, you need someone solid to grab onto. Bono sings,

> Feel like I'm fallin'
> I'm spinnin' on a wheel
> It always stops beside a name
> A presence I can feel.

Jesus, the name above all names, is right there beside you.

A friend in Birmingham described her experience of the presence she could feel in the midst of her life's conditionality. She's been diagnosed with cancer, although she is relatively young. She wrote,

> Around 6:15 Friday evening, home alone and putzing in my pantry, I noticed a tightness in my lower back, so I started walking toward my living room to lie down on the floor and take care of it. In the passage between the two rooms, I felt my heart crack wide open, and I was overcome with love. I have no other way to explain it. I was flooded with an overwhelming sense of joy, love, being completely and fully held. By so many. In that moment I believe that I experienced the infinite possibility of love. I got myself down on the floor, on my back, arms outstretched and soaked it in. I was sobbing, not out of fear or sadness, but out of gratitude for what is coming my way.

Jesus resists the devil's temptations, but the devil returns to Jesus at an opportune time. That opportune time is Good Friday, when Jesus willingly plunges headlong into the fault line of the world's sin and misery. As Jesus dies, the devil licks his chops, thinking he has pulled a fast one on God. The Son of God, dead! But something deeper is at work. Jesus is raised from the dead on the first Easter Sunday. He is solid enough for Thomas to touch.

As we prayed in the collect for today, Jesus is "mighty to save." His death and resurrection assert God's love for you once and for all. There is no if-then, no conditionality in Jesus. Without stipulations, he declares to you, "I am with you always, to the end of the age."

Amen.

February 21, 2016 ‡ *Second Sunday in Lent (C)*

A Fox in the Henhouse

LUKE 13:31-35

C hristie was given a chicken coop for a birthday present about 10 years ago. It's in our backyard. Most years we buy spring chicks, just hatched, and put them in an incubator in the basement. Last year, we got 21 eggs shipped to us to incubate in the Christ Church Preschool. It's very exciting when they hatch, but the problem with chicks and eggs is that you don't know if they will be hens or roosters.

We live in a neighborhood off Rugby Road, so roosters are not an option if we don't want our neighbors to hate us. We want hens because they cluck around, are very low maintenance, and lay eggs. Roosters wake up the neighborhood at 5 am. Plus, they are a little scary.

We like to have five or six hens at a time. But we have to replenish the brood most years because even though we live in the city, predators abound. Raccoons, for instance, are very interested in the chickens. Sometimes they will get into the coop through an unknown tear in the chicken wire. Hawks are on the alert when we let the chickens go free range in the back yard during the day. The wiliest and most beautiful predator is, of course, the fox. Sometimes early in the morning we'll hear a ruckus in the hen house and discover a red fox circling the coop.

Perhaps you noticed two of the aforementioned creatures in this morning's Gospel reading. The Pharisees warn Jesus that Herod wants to kill him. Jesus responds, "Go and tell that fox for me, 'Listen, I am casting out demons and performing cures today and tomorrow, and on the third day I finish my work." In that context, calling somebody a fox was a major insult. A fox was someone of unscrupulous character, merciless and self-seeking.

You may remember that Herod's father, also named Herod, tried to murder Jesus as an infant. Anxious about the rumors of a newborn king, he issued the decree for the Slaughter of the Innocents, the killing of every male Hebrew child under 3 years old. Apparently, the apple hasn't fallen far from the tree.

Jesus isn't too worried about Herod's impending threat, but it does turn his mind toward Jerusalem. He "hear[s] Jerusalem bells a-ringing." But the Jerusalem bells toll mournfully. Jesus laments, "Jerusalem, Jerusalem, the city that kills the prophets and stones those who are sent to it! How often have I desired to gather your children together as a hen gathers her brood under her wings, and you were not willing!"

Jesus knows that the actual threat to his life lies in Jerusalem, the "city that kills the prophets." The irony is thick: the epicenter of worship for God's chosen people is also the graveyard of God's messengers. But instead of responding in anger, Jesus responds in mercy, wishing to "gather your children together as a hen gathers her brood under her wings."

Jesus as protective hen is one of the great feminine images of God in the scripture. But it is also an odd one, isn't it? When a fox gets into the hen house, the hen is defenseless. This happened to our chickens several years ago—carnage everywhere. Christie had to deal with it because I was on a fishing trip in Montana. That was not a high point in our marriage.

Why does Jesus choose a hen as an image of his protective care? Why not become the lion of Judah or the fierce eagle of Exodus? Even a rooster stands a better chance against a fox than a hen does. Barbara Brown Taylor comments on this. I'll quote her at some length because she's so good:

A hen is what Jesus chooses, which—if you think about it— is pretty typical of him. He is always turning things upside down, so that children and peasants wind up on top while kings and scholars land on the bottom. He is always wrecking our expectations of how things should turn out by giving prizes to losers and paying the last first. So of course he chooses a chicken, which is about as far from a fox as you can get. That way the options become very clear: you can live by licking your chops or you can die protecting the chicks.

This week I came across an arresting example of a hen sheltering her brood in a time of death. NBA basketball coach Monty Williams gave a powerful testimony at his wife's funeral. She was killed by a reckless driver, leaving Williams with five children to raise alone. His remarks are filled with faith and forgiveness. But what caught my attention was an incident that happened two years ago.

One of his players, Ryan Anderson, discovered his girlfriend's body after her suicide. Obviously devastated, he called his coach. A *Sports Illustrated* article captures the awful scene:

> Pelicans coach Monty Williams hurrying in with a team security guard and finding Ryan slumped on the carpet, his back to the door, unable to rise. Williams dropping to his knees and hugging his player, the two men rocking back and forth.
>
> …
>
> As they drove in silence, Williams kept thinking that it was fine if he blew a game, but he couldn't mess up now. Once home, he huddled with his wife, Ingrid, and Ryan in the family room, praying. Ingrid's brother had committed suicide recently. She knew not to say it was going to be OK, because it wasn't. "This is going to be hard for a long time," she told Ryan.
>
> That night, as the family pastor came and went, Ryan cried so much that it felt as if he were dry heaving or bleeding internally. Each convulsion ripped his insides apart. Around 1 am, at Ingrid's urging, Monty brought one of his sons' mattresses down to the living room. There the two men lay

through the night, Ryan curled on the sofa and his coach on the floor next to him. When Ryan wanted to talk, they talked. Otherwise there was only his muted sobbing. Finally, just after the sun came up, Ryan fell into a fitful sleep.

Coach Williams didn't stop the terrible thing from happening, but he tenderly sheltered his suffering player during the worst of it. When bad things happen, I sure long for a Lion of Judah to come kill all my enemies, a superhero God to vanquish the bad guys. But God, the God we know in Jesus, has other means and methods.

Taylor says,

> Jesus won't be king of the jungle in this or any other story. What he will be is a mother hen, who stands between the chicks and those who mean to do them harm. She has no fangs, no claws, no rippling muscles. All she has is her willingness to shield her babies with her own body. If the fox wants them, he will have to kill her first.
>
> Which he does, as it turns out.

When Jesus does get to Jerusalem, when the people on Palm Sunday cry out, "Blessed is the one who comes in the name of the Lord!"—when Palm Sunday gives way to the Last Supper and to Good Friday—the fox goes after the hen. Jesus is in the city that kills the prophets.

In the Garden of Gethsemane, the fox comes for the hen.

> He slides up on her one night in the yard while all the babies are asleep. When her cry wakens them, they scatter. She dies the next day where both foxes and chickens can see her— wings spread, breast exposed—without a single chick beneath her feathers. It breaks her heart, but it does not change a thing. If you mean what you say, then this is how you stand.

Jesus says to tell that fox that "on the third day I finish my work." And sure enough, he cries from the cross, "It is finished." Jesus' death on our behalf has protected us from the judgment we deserve. His sheltering wings have become his outstretched arms on the cross, so that the whole world might be drawn to him. I'll close with the final prayer of our Good Friday service: "Lord Jesus Christ, Son of the living God, we pray you to set your passion, cross, and death between your judgment and our souls, now and in the hour of our death. Give mercy and grace to the living; pardon and rest to the dead."

Amen.

February 20, 2005 ‡ *Second Sunday in Lent (A)*

You Must Be Born Again

JOHN 3:1-16

This morning in the Gospel we meet a man in a crisis. Nicodemus comes to Jesus by cover of night in a crisis. The resulting conversation is magnificent.

Nicodemus is in a crisis of faith. He is a Pharisee, a member of the Jewish ruling council, a Bible scholar, and a pillar of society. He's got everything going for him that you can imagine in worldly terms and also in religious terms. But obviously something's missing.

Maybe he felt that gnawing anxiety that many of us feel when we know there is something missing. Maybe he woke up in the night, staring into the dark, and reviewed his life: Marriage, kids, and grandkids are all doing fine. Job is fairly secure. Portfolio could be better, but we're not headed to the poorhouse. Maybe he woke up in the dark and thought, *I think I'm OK with God. After all, religion is very important to me: I've been an Episcopalian all my life, baptized and confirmed, served on the vestry, even taught Sunday School, but why am I waking up in the dark and why does it feel like something's missing?*

There must have been an inner conversation as disorienting as this to drive a person like Nicodemus to an uneducated, itinerant preacher-slash-miracle-worker in the middle of the night, when no one could see him. Nicodemus is a ruler of Israel. This wayfaring prophet should be asking Nicodemus questions about faith, not vice versa. Yet there he is, in the dark with Jesus, because deep down Nicodemus suspects that his own faith is *inadequate*.

Have you ever felt this? Have you ever asked yourself, "Is my faith adequate? Do I have the faith that is necessary?" Has this worry every awakened you in the dark? Or if it hasn't, maybe it's the kind of ultimate question that *should* awaken you in the dark. Are you OK with God? That's what's driving Nicodemus to Jesus. Are you OK with God? Before you answer that question, listen in to what took place that night.

Nicodemus comes to Jesus and, like people in crisis, makes no small talk. He doesn't even apologize for showing up after hours. His need is great; he gets right to it. He says, "I've seen the miracles. Who are you?" Jesus' response is very quirky. He doesn't do anything to comfort this man in crisis or assure him or relieve the tension.

In reply, Jesus declares, "Very truly, I tell you, no one can see the kingdom of God without being born from above." Instead of giving Nicodemus a pat answer, he gives him a cryptic one. Jesus doesn't let Nicodemus off the hook with something like "It's OK, God loves you," or "Well, Nicodemus, your faith is fine and don't worry because we're all on a journey anyway." Instead, he heightens Nicodemus' sense of crisis; he insists that Nicodemus grapple with this spiritual angst and blindness. He says to the man born with every worldly and spiritual privilege, *You must be born again.*

You must be born again. It's a phrase that sends chills up the spine of every proper Episcopalian. It's a phrase that sends Nicodemus into even deeper crisis and confusion. He asks, "Can one enter a second time into the mother's womb and be born?" He takes the command literally. What does Jesus mean when he says, *You must be born again?*

To get at this, let's put the emphasis on two different words in the command. First put the emphasis on *must—You* must *be born again.* There are no exceptions to the necessity of new birth. It doesn't matter who you are, what you've done or not done. Our Lord says that everyone *must* be born again.

Van Morrison is one of my favorite singers. But I have to disagree with Van when he once said in an interview, "I don't need to be born again because I was born right the first time." If there was anyone born right the first time it was Nicodemus. He was "of the seed of Abraham," a moral, upright man who taught the Hebrew Scriptures. He was a ruler of Israel. In God's terms, you can't get any more "born right the first time" than that. Yet Jesus tells him that he *must* be born again.

Why? Because he was born a murderer? Born on the wrong side of the tracks? No, because the first time he was born a *human being*! As we read in verse 6, "What is born of the flesh is flesh." We were not born right the first time. Our flesh is fallen. When Adam fell, he didn't just break his big toe and need a little pain medicine and a crutch to get better. When he fell he broke his neck and was utterly ruined! In our flesh, in our natural birth, "there is no health in us," as one collect from our prayer book puts it.

That's why Jesus speaks in such extreme terms. Note the verbs in verses 3 and 5. Unless you're born again, you'll never *see* the Kingdom of God and you'll never *enter* it, either. That is to say, the first time around we are *blind* and *powerless*. Everybody is. No exceptions. Remember, Nicodemus came to Jesus at night, literally. John uses the darkness metaphorically all through his Gospel to symbolize the spiritual blindness and darkness of every human being. We are born spiritually blind, spiritually powerless. It sounds strange to say it, but we're born *dead*. No wonder Nicodemus was in a faith crisis.

I must say that I hope that this is gnawing at you a little right now, making you ask the question that Nicodemus is asking: Is my faith adequate? Am I really a Christian? In his love for Nicodemus, Jesus pushed him to that place. I hope you'll go to that place this morning.

If we're born blind, powerless, dead the first time around, then what must happen? Now we'll put the emphasis on the second part. Jesus says, *you must be born again*. Think about the metaphor for a second. There must be regeneration, total transformation, new creation, a total change of nature.

Reformation, moral change, amendment of the old man is not adequate. If you have faith in any kind of self-improvement, then your faith is inadequate. It underestimates the extent of your deadness. We must be born anew. This speaks of Tennyson's famous sigh "And ah for a man to arise in me, / That the man I am may cease to be." Nicodemus had the beginnings of that sigh in him—that's what drove him to Jesus in the night. *Ah for a new man (or woman) to arise in me, that the blind, powerless, dead one may cease to be.*

This being born again is total newness, and it happens totally outside ourselves. There's a lot of Bible-Belt baggage that goes along with the term "born again." Let me be clear: being born again is not "making a decision for Jesus." We are "born from above," as the Greek can also be translated. It's a top-down act. We've got nothing to do with it. Dead people can't make decisions. Think. Did you have anything to do with your physical birth? Jesus is intentional in his use of the metaphor. So it's the same with your spiritual birth. Being born again is an act of the Holy Spirit, who is "the Lord, the giver of life," as we say in the creed. You don't come to Jesus to be born again; dead people can't go anywhere. There are no "dead men walking." Jesus must come to you.

Six people drowned in rip tides off the Gulf coast last summer. A boy on a surfboard saw one of the dead men floating out past the breakers. He paddled up and tried to shake the drowned man. Obviously, the dead man was in no position to hear the boy's pleas and decide to be undead. He needed total new life from the outside. So it is with us. We are not alive until we are *made* alive by the Lord and Giver of Life. So, as Jesus says, why are you surprised that I say, *You must be born again*? Isn't it obvious?

So where are we left? As a preacher, I'm in the odd position of feebly imitating the words of my Lord as I tell you, You must be born again. I hope you feel the urgency. But since the work of forming new life in dead people is the sovereign work of God, you are in no position to rebirth yourselves. This is what Nicodemus was faced with. What happened to him?

Fast forward to the end of the Gospel. When Jesus died on the cross, who was there to take his body down? None other than Nicodemus. The man who came to Jesus by night in a crisis came to Jesus by day in love to tend to Jesus' dead body. He was a changed man; a new man had arisen in him. How? As he looked up to his dead Lord on the cross, surely he must have had echoing in his mind the words of his first conversation with Jesus, words that now made some kind of sense: "For God so loved the world that he gave his only Son, so that everyone who believes in him may not perish but may have eternal life."

God says through the prophet Hosea, "My people are destroyed for lack of knowledge." This morning, in this magnificent scripture, we're given knowledge, knowledge of our deadness and knowledge of the Lord who gives new birth. I pray that each of you this morning will first look at your own blindness, powerlessness, and deadness. And I pray that each of you will look at Jesus Christ lifted up on the cross for you. And I pray that the Holy Spirit, the Lord and Giver of Life, will breath into your dead hearts so that you may say, "Yes, Lord, I believe," and that you may not perish, but have everlasting life.

Amen.

March 10, 2013 ‡ *Fourth Sunday in Lent (C)*

Semiotic Grace: The Word Beneath our Words

LUKE 15:1-3, 11B-32

I f you are someone who loses your temper, or says things you don't mean, or says mean things that you do actually mean, or wishes you had said something in response to someone and then rehearses at night all the little speeches you would like to deliver—if you are someone who talks to anyone about anything, then I hope this sermon will give you some help and some hope.

There is a *New Yorker* cartoon of a husband and wife in the middle of a heated argument, the husband stiff and arms crossed in a chair, the wife standing over him, elbows out. The caption reads, "Let's stop this before we both say a lot of things we mean!"

Saying things we mean is harder than we think. Think about all the times you've said what you don't mean to say, times when you've been misunderstood or misinterpreted. How many times in your own arguments do you say, "I didn't mean that," or, "You're not hearing what I'm saying"?

And as we get older, we can no longer remember what it is we even want to say or the words to use to say it! As an aging friend said recently, life becomes a guessing game of charades. We couldn't think of the word "sushi" the other day, so we resorted to "you know, raw fish with rice and really hot green stuff." I've been having so-called "senior moments" since I was about 18.

When you think for a minute about the frailty and susceptibility of language, then you wonder how anyone communicates with anyone at all. When you think of a word being a *signifier* of some object, like the word "tree" for what you think of as a tree, then you realize the journey that communication requires, and it's no wonder we have difficulty getting our meaning across.

First you've got to think about the words that suit your meaning (let's say you decide on "tree"), then you speak the word. Then the person you're talking to has to hear what you say, and at last she has to reinterpret the meaning according to her understanding of "tree." When you throw in modifiers like *"cherry tree"* or *"old-growth forest* tree," you muddle things up further.

But "tree" is easily compared to conceptual words like "truth" or "humility" or "desire." What I mean by truth, even if *I* know what I mean by truth, may have no connection whatsoever with what *you* mean by truth. In so many cases, "what we've got here is a failure to communicate."

Then when you factor in all the subconscious psychological influences in any given conversation—the latent grudges, the just-under-the-surface bigotries, the fact that something about her reminds you of your mother or your rascal stepson, not to mention the libidinal heat that smolders in every direction—then any mutually understood meaningful bridge between any two people becomes nothing short of a miracle. We need grace in our attempts at meaning-making, in our *semiotics*.

I'm trying to explain a simple version of *deconstruction*. Deconstructionists believe that everyone is so steeped in his or her own experience that no signifier, no word, could be coupled with whatever it is trying to signify, to point at. Order and mutual understanding is elusive. There just are no still points of meaning in a turning world.

Faulkner named his first masterpiece *The Sound and the Fury*, from Macbeth's speech that life is nothing more than "a tale / Told by an idiot, full of sound and fury, / Signifying nothing." Later in life, Faulkner called the book his "most splendid failure." Recognizing the limits of language—about which, ironically, I'm preaching—he believed that every book fails to truthfully communicate what the author intends. But *The Sound and the Fury* came the closest.

Purposely, the central figure is Benjy, an "idiot," who speaks without reference to time. As my friend James Wilson says, Benjy's incessant moaning, howling, and screaming is the "sound and fury" which becomes the background noise of the entire novel.

Benjy's example is obviously extreme, but it points to our shared condition as people: much of what we do and say is full of sound and fury, signifying nothing. Just look at Congress. Or just look at your own family.

It takes its toll. When I speak in anger at my son or in judgment at Christie, even when I long to communicate love and grace, I widen the gulf between us. Marriages fall apart because men and women cannot talk about sex or money or children. It's terrible to go to bed with unresolved conflict; one never sleeps well.

This grim reality puts in profound relief the miracle of any kind of meaningful, and hopefully loving, connection with anyone else, as well as our total need for help. We need someone or something else to give significance to our signifiers, to give meaning to our words, to give us still points in a turning world. After all, we just prayed in our collect last week that "we have no power in ourselves to help ourselves."

Our story from Scripture this morning delivers this help. It is one of the best-known stories told by the divine storyteller and surely the one that tells us all we really need to know about God. The story is the Prodigal Son, of course. It might also be known as the Gracious Father, for in the end, the story Jesus tells is about God's grace. I want to focus on one part of this story: the son's speech to his love-struck father upon his return from derelict living. All the while, I want to keep in mind the hobbled efficacy of talk, which is limp at best. Maybe that's where the maxim emerged: talk is cheap.

The prodigal son's talk was cheap. The fact is that he had spent all his money on profligate living and found himself close to dying. Only then does it occur to him to go back to his father. His apology is just his playing the only card he had left. And it's pretty lame: "Father, I have sinned against heaven and before you; I am no longer worthy to be called your son; treat me like one of your hired hands." Granted, the content seems sound enough, but I would guess the tone was robotic. It may have sounded like siblings who are forced by parents to apologize to one another after fighting: "So-rry." The signifier is totally detached from any real meaning. Perhaps more to the point, he wouldn't have said anything at all if he still had two nickels to rub together.

Here's the astonishing thing: It just doesn't matter that the son's talk was nothing but sound and fury. It appears that the father didn't even hear it! He was out of breath from sprinting out to meet his bedraggled boy and caught up in the chorus of joy beating in his heart.

It's doubtful that the boy returned with "true faith and hearty repentance," as we say in the preface to our absolution. But it doesn't matter, just as the fact that none of us ever really has perfectly true faith or perfectly hearty repentance. What matters is the father's forgiveness and absolution, which depends entirely on him.

It's God who gives meaning to our sound and our fury. It's God who takes the fractured talk between people and makes the miracle of real connection. The Tower of Babel, the first deconstructionist story, is not the end of the story.

There is also the story of the Word, who was in the beginning with God, who is God and who was made flesh, and who told a story to the hearts of all who long for Love to throw his arms around us and throw a party for us, too, even when we can't or don't say what we mean. Or when we *do* say, unfortunately, *exactly* what we mean. I've got to believe that Jesus drives the train of our talk and is the track laid down for its passage. The semiotic grace is this: there is a Word beneath our words.

Philip Yancey talks about a small town orchestra's version of Beethoven's Ninth, an obviously sublime symphony. The orchestra's attempt is, quite frankly, not very good. But don't blame Beethoven because the orchestra struggles. As Yancey points out, that ensemble's version may be the only Beethoven some Coloradans will ever hear. And like our talk, our repentance, our attempts to communicate, it's good enough. God's grace permeates our failure to communicate. It's that deep. In God's gracious ears, he hears a masterpiece in our splendid failure.

Addie Bundren, the nihilistic mother in Faulkner's *As I Lay Dy-*

ing, says, "people to whom sin is just a matter of words, to them salvation is just words too." The Word made flesh, who told the story of God's grace, tells us that salvation is more than words. Do you wonder where the Christ figure is in the story of the Prodigal Son? He is in the fatted calf that was sacrificed, so the family could come together, to drink and laugh and celebrate and talk with meaning and with love.

Amen.

March 19, 2007 ‡ *Monday after the Fourth Sunday in Lent (C)*
Anglican College Ministry

Family First

MARK 3:31-35

A *rrested Development* is an anointed television show. Outside the canon of Scripture, and possibly Shakespeare, parts of Freud, and most U2 songs, *Arrested Development* wins the prize for the most Holy Spirit-inspired media. Do you really think it is a *coincidence* that Jesus ministered for 3 years and Arrested Development ran for 3 years before they were both canceled?

Arrested Development is at its funniest and truest when centered on family conflict, which is most of the time. The characters are caricatures of neediness, self-centeredness, psychosexual desire, and myopia. Yet who doesn't recognize family members in the characters? And if you've had some therapy, then you're able to recognize yourself too. The family members are always in exaggerated conflict, but their motto is "Family First."

Family First. Most people, no matter how dysfunctional their family of origin is, will recognize that this is the way that most of the world operates. Blood is thicker than water. Blood kinship is the strongest. If you've spent any time in non-Western cultures you will have discovered this. You may make what you think is a close friend, but your friend's sister always trumps you. This is a near universal truth, whether you're in Mexico or Alaska or Zanzibar: it's always *Family First.*

This is true in much of Western culture, too. And not just with Big-Fat-Greek-Wedding Americans or rural Americans. Virginians have their own type of Family First mythology. We always want to know who your grandfather was. One "First Family" of Virginia mother told her son, "Make sure you don't marry anyone whose last name ends in a vowel." She didn't want the blue blood to be mixed with someone—God forbid—non-Anglo-Saxon! Family First. In this case, *First Family First.*

It seems only right and good and natural to "focus on the family," doesn't it? They are the people who know you. They are the people who are supposed to love you. They are the ones who have to take you in when you come out of rehab. They are the ones whose ties are stronger than choice. The claims of your nuclear family, the claims of your family of origin, are universally natural, normal, and undeniable. It's Family.

Well, if you listened to the Gospel reading, you know where we're headed with this one. From the very beginning, Jesus of Nazareth destroys the very notion of *Family First.* He reveals it as a destructive mythology. He pulls back the curtain on this idol worshipped almost universally that seems to come so naturally to us.

What Jesus does in today's Gospel is shocking. If you think you have a tight family, think again in light of first-century Jewish culture. Your family was your identity and your security. Your family was also your destiny. Your family determined what you would do (why do you think Jesus was a carpenter?) and where you would live. Jesus' family of origin was no different. (Mary was a Jewish mother.)

So when Mary and her other sons show up at the door of a house where Jesus is teaching, they expect to have front row seats. Instead, they can't get in. And when someone tells Jesus that his mother and his brothers are outside waiting for him, imagine what they must think when Jesus says, "Who are my mother and my brothers?" And imagine the shock and horror of what happens next: "And looking at those who sat around him, he said, 'Here are my mother and my brothers! Whoever does the will of God is my brother and sister and mother.'"

Jesus' family must think that he is out of his mind talking like that. Well, that's exactly what they do think. If we look back a few verses we see that "they went out to restrain him, for people were saying, 'He has gone out of his mind.'"

Hearing this rumor, "the Family" (it sounds like *The Godfather*) comes to do a kind of intervention, like when someone has an addiction and their relatives come to take control. This is what Jesus' family tries to do, probably because of the way he has been breaking all the religious taboos, healing on the Sabbath and hanging out with prostitutes and outcasts and other sketchy people.

But when they show up to take charge, he breaks the even deeper taboo of Family First. Right in front of his mother and his brothers he looks at the hooker and calls her his mother and the sketchy guy and calls him his brother and the unclean woman and calls her his sister. Do you hear how scandalous this is? No wonder people wanted to kill Jesus so early on in his ministry.

There are several ways we could go with this sermon right now. Some of you are establishing your own independence from your family mythology, and it's causing trouble on the home front. Maybe they feel you are out of your mind and they need to do an intervention. You live in tension when you go home because you're not the person you were and yet you revert to the person you were when you're home. As a result, you dread being with them again.

I think the moment that a boy becomes a man is the moment that he can speak openly about his own thoughts and ideas to his father. This can happen at 12 or 21 or 42 or 64 or, sadly, never at all. (I'm not sure what the female corollary is to this: please tell me.) This transition moment happens as the old family mythology is confronted and exposed in the presence of the patriarch. This is a highly fraught, deeply anxious moment, especially when the mythology is thick and layered. As Faulkner famously said, "The past is never dead. It's not even past." This transitional, growing up moment is the fecund place of great art, great literature, great comedy, great music, and all psychotherapy.

Jesus had his moment at 12 years old when he stayed in the Temple in Jerusalem while his family left to return to Nazareth. He didn't even tell anyone! And when they returned all anxious and worried and found him in the Temple, he said, "Why did you worry? This is where I belong—in my Father's house." And if that moment had been forgotten, here at 33 years old, he leaves no doubt about what he thinks about Family First.

Some of you are very nervous right now because you come from what seems to be a good and healthy family, and this iconoclastic language from the pulpit is unsettling. But what's more unsettling is that it's right there in Jesus' mouth. As I say every week, I'm not making this up.

Some of you are parents, and you live your lives through your children. You think what you feel is love, but in fact it smothers and depresses your children. Some of you are trying to make sense of divorce or death. Some of you just coexist with your family when you have to and are resigned to the distance that divides. The luckier among you will turn the turmoil into creativity and create a sequel to *Arrested Development*. And as we said a few weeks ago, the rest of you just move to Oregon.

No matter what your situation, what unites us is the gargantuan influence of Family First. Freud said that your life is basically determined by how you were loved or not loved from birth to age 6. You can agree or disagree with him, but who can question the all-consuming influence of your family of origin?

Where is the good news tonight? We've seen a pattern in this Mark preaching series. Jesus destroys a thing in order to create a new thing. Last week Justin preached so powerfully about Jesus destroying the distorted view of the Sabbath in order to create a place of real freedom and rest.

Tonight is no different. Jesus is not anti-family, but he is anti-Family First. His focus is not on the family, at least not in the idolatrous ways of most people. By destroying the mythology of Family First, Jesus gives us back the family in a way that is good and right and life-giving. When an idol dies, the thing is given back the due worth it deserves.

Jesus doesn't abandon his family, even though they want to institutionalize him in the beginning. At the end, when Mary stands at the cross of her bleeding and dying Son, Jesus takes care of her. He makes sure that John will look after her when Jesus is no longer around. In this way, Jesus obeys the Fifth Commandment to honor his father and his mother.

How does this deconstruction of Family First idolatry actually happen? First by calling a thing what it is, by speaking the truth about your family life, come what may. But this can only happen when there is a prior claim on your life, when you have come to see that God is your Father, and those around you who have been forgiven and redeemed are your true brothers and sisters. The destructive grip of Family First loses its power when you can see, as John says in his prologue, "to all who received him, who believed in his name, he gave power to become children of God, who were born, not of blood or of the will of the flesh or of the will of man, but of God." In God's view, blood is thicker than water. Not the blood of kinship, but the blood of Christ, shed to make men and women brothers and sisters of a loving Father.

And those who have believed in him may even include some from your family of origin. Jesus' blood covers them too: In this case your father is your brother, your daughter is your sister. You can actually love each other on equal footing, rather than by the rules of patrimony or family identity. You can rejoice in your family as a collection of equally needy, equally broken, equally developmentally arrested, and equally redeemed sinners, covered by the blood that is truly thicker than water.

And if some of your kin are not believers, at least as far as you can see, perhaps you'll be able to see that since you were saved by grace, you may be able to treat them with the same grace and forgiveness with which God has treated you.

Jesus refuses Family First because he wants to break down exclusive barriers and to open the doors for everyone, including the dirty and the sketchy. His blood was not shed just for his blood kin. His blood was shed for everyone, or, as we say in our communion prayer, "for the sins of the whole world." This is incredible news for the lonely and the hurt and the orphaned and the widowed. No matter how wounded you've been by your own Family First mythology, Jesus has taken you in: "And looking about at those who sat around him, he said, 'Here are my mothers and my brothers! Whoever does the will of God, he is my brother and sister and mother.'"

Amen.

March 21, 2010 ‡ *Fifth Sunday in Lent (C)*

What Real Love Looks Like

JOHN 12:1-8

As we just passed the Ides of March last week, I reread *Julius Caesar*, a play about someone who did not take note of that day and so was murdered March 15, 44 BC. As always, Shakespeare delivers keen insight into human nature, in this case, the nature of real love.

After Caesar's death, Brutus is sorting out his rearranged relationships; those who are still love him after he assassinates Caesar, and those who have grown distant. Brutus asks Lucilius how a friend has reacted to him, and he responds:

> *Lucilius*
> With courtesy and with respect enough;
> But not with such familiar instances,
> Nor with such free and friendly conference,
> As he hath used of old.

> *Brutus*
> Thou has described
> A hot friend cooling: ever note, Lucilius,
> When love begins to sicken and decay,

It useth an enforced ceremony.

Haven't you experienced that, on the giving and the receiving ends? When you are close to someone and there is a rupture in your relationship and you both know it, it just becomes awkward. You don't really know how to make the transition from closeness to distance, so you use the forms of closeness ("enforced ceremony") without the real heart and emotion in it ("free and friendly conference"). Sometimes this takes the form of over-exuberance to cover up the awkwardness: "HEY! SO GREAT TO SEE YOU! SORRY I HAVEN'T CALLED! HOW ARE YOU!"

Enforced ceremony, courtesy, and respect are just not enough to sustain real love. There's nothing wrong with ceremony, courtesy, and respect, of course. It's just that when they are devoid of real substance they become useless or worse.

You can often see this dynamic played out in grandparent-grandchild relationships. You can tell the grandparents who light up when they see their grandchildren. They don't "babysit." They just love to be with their grandchildren. You can usually tell the quality of real love between the grandparents and grandchildren by the goofiness of the grandparental names. Grown adults who delight in being called names like "Ging Ging" and "Poo Pa" are grandparents who are free and friendly with their grandchildren. Whatever the 2-year-old names you is music to your ears.

I saw my one grandmother once a year at Thanksgiving. She was a very formal lady, whose visits required lots of enforced ceremony. We called her "Grandmother Walker." She did send me 100 dollars every Christmas, however, which in my mind more than compensated for the enforced ceremony!

In today's Gospel, we have a beautiful scene of real love expressed to Jesus. It is a free and friendly, unselfconscious kind of love. It is the kind of love that is not aware of anybody else, not aware of any rules or ceremony, not even aware of itself. It is unmeditated; its left hand does not know what it's right hand is doing. It is the kind of love that is only aware of its object.

Mary expresses her love for Jesus in an extraordinary way. It's the kind of love without which Christianity is just a religion of form without substance. Going to church is just an obligation. It's like kissing your sister. Unless your heart is totally involved with a kind of unselfconscious love, then it really is better just to bag it. I really mean that! I want you to come to church not out of enforced ceremony, but out of real love for God. This is the point of worship.

Mary show us what real love looks like. Martha and Mary are giving a dinner party in Jesus' honor. The occasion? He had just raised their brother Lazarus from the dead. It must have been happy and filled with extremely interesting conversation: "So, uh, Lazarus, where exactly did you go while you were dead for four days? Did you happen to see Uncle Manny while you were there? Jesus, have you raised anyone else from the dead lately? My mother-in-law died last Tuesday, but no need to bother with her."

They were all reclining at the table as was the Jewish custom: a long low table, some pillows nearby, everybody eating and drinking, when a very strange thing happens. Martha is serving, of course. Mary disappears and returns with some perfume. Jesus would have been lying down, his head near the dinner table, his feet away. Mary comes and anoints Jesus' feet with the perfume. As she does, she breaches ceremony and creates a big scene.

Now, why is this a scene? It was a normal part of Jewish hospitality to offer people some kind of aromatherapy as they came into your home because people generally smelled bad. Yet this was a scene. The version of this story in Mark says that Mary was "scolded." Why?

The dinner party was totally disrupted because of Mary's expression of love for Jesus. It was an embarrassing, over-the-top display. It was not "all things in moderation." I think it is the essence of real love: desire rather than obligation.

What about her love makes it real? For one thing, she doesn't count the cost. She gets the nard out of the family safe deposit box. This was the family heirloom. This was by far the most expensive thing that they owned. It probably represented 90 percent of their wealth. This "pound of costly perfume made of pure nard" was their stock, their bond, their CD, their IRA, their trust fund, their life insurance, their health insurance, their inheritance, and their legacy.

And what does Mary do? In the other Gospel accounts, she breaks the jar open and dumps it all out over Jesus' head and then anoints his feet with the overflow. It's like taking a million dollars in cash and burning it in the fireplace to keep Jesus warm.

Not only does Mary not count the cost, but her real love doesn't stand on her rights. Mary anoints Jesus' feet. This is an extremely demeaning act, like scrubbing toilets, only worse. Feet smelled. Feet still smell. When I was in college, a guy in my dorm used to put his shoes out in the hall because his roommate wouldn't allow them in their room. The problem is that the hall smelled terrible all the time.

Who wants to deal with somebody else's feet? Nobody. For instance, in biblical times, slaves had no rights. But Jewish slaves did have one right. They were not forced to touch anyone's feet. That was too demeaning, even for a slave. So what does Mary do at the dinner party? She surrenders her rights and anoints Jesus' feet.

Mary also doesn't care what anyone else thinks, another mark of real love. We know this because when Mary anoints Jesus' feet, she wipes his feet with her hair. To do that, she does something scandalous in Jewish society: she unbinds her hair and lets it down. Only harlots did this. A woman never "let her hair down" in public, as the saying still goes. According to Jewish law, a woman could be stoned for doing such an intimate and scandalous act.

She must have been nearly prostrate, too, in order to wipe Jesus' feet. Talk about unselfconscious! A public display of affection! She is consumed with her love and gratitude for the one who raised her brother from the dead. The people who were concerned with enforced ceremony blew their tops and harshly rebuked her. Jesus responds, "Leave her alone." According to Matthew, he even said, "Truly I tell you, wherever this good news is proclaimed in the whole world, what she has done will be told in remembrance of her."

Is your love for Jesus like that? Not conditioned by cost, by right, by what others think? I would sure like my love for God and for others to be like that. What could possibly motivate a love like that? A love for Christ where you give it all away, where you don't even think about what is owed you, and you couldn't care less what other people think. There is no obligation there, but only desire. Again, what could possibly motivate a love like that?

Think about Mary for a second. Where is Mary whenever we

see her? She's at Jesus' feet, listening to his teaching. She's soaking up all he has to say, everything about him. She just witnessed Jesus raising her brother from death and had an intense conversation with Jesus about death and resurrection. Mary is deeply aware of what Jesus has done and what he soon must do. Remember that this party is on the Saturday before Holy Week. She knows that Good Friday is coming. Verse 7 is the key: "She bought it so that she might keep it for the day of my burial." Mary is anointing her Lord's body for the grave.

Do you hear this? At this festive dinner party, Mary is preparing Jesus for the cross. She knew that he must die, and my guess is that she knew that he must die for her. Although she couldn't name it, she understood what we call the substitutionary atonement: Christ died for you. It must have melted her heart.

But Mary saw it, and it caused her to love with abandon. When you see it, it will cause you to love with abandon, too. Desire comes from a melted heart. You can't lecture people into it, you can't legislate it, and no enforced ceremony can make it happen. Only the cross of Christ can melt your heart, when you know that Jesus Christ went to the cross for you personally. This is why we always say, "The body of Christ given for you," and, "The blood of Christ shed for you."

There is one more thing to say. The perfume was so sweet and potent that the smell would have stayed on Jesus' body all week, all through his beatings, his mocking, his scourging, his stripping, and his nailing on the cross. Her act makes his death sweet. Perhaps it brought him some comfort, this sensory recall of her love and devotion. This love is what he desired from Mary. This love is what he desires from you—a love that knows no cost, that considers no rights, that overflows the stern banks of ceremony despite the rebuke of others. A love that is generated by him and for him, a love whose heartbeat is the cross of Christ.

Amen.

March 16, 2008 ‡ *Palm Sunday (A)*

No Defense

MATTHEW 27:11-54

I want to look briefly this morning at our Gospel account of Jesus' trial before Pilate. Jesus is arrested, accused, bound, and delivered over to Pilate. As he stands before Pilate, the chief priests, and the elders, his life hangs in the balance.

Accused of blasphemy and facing execution, Jesus is asked to defend himself, to give an account to explain himself, or else he will face crucifixion. What happens next is what one of our ministry interns called "one of the most deafening sounds in all of Scripture."

But before we get to Jesus' response, think for a second what it is like to be accused. It was in the headlines last week, of course. Governor Eliot Spitzer of New York sat in the hot seat trying to give an account of himself. His wife, one article said, stood inches away but never touched him. His enemies and accusers popped champagne and gloated with glee. One said, "I have never had any doubt about his lack of character and integrity—and he's proven me correct." Witty, but devastating.

Commentator Cal Thomas joined the fun, saying that Spitzer's wife shouldn't stick by him during the press conferences and citing all kinds of Bible passages about adultery. Spitzer should have known better, apparently, because it's all there in black and white.

He concluded his article with an ominous whammy from the book of Numbers: "Be sure your sin will find you out."

I'm sure you've been on both sides of the hot seat. You've been the one who gloats at another's downfall, accusing and then delighting in the accuracy of the accusation. But if you've been around the block once or twice, you've also been the one who is accused. You've been the one who is asked to defend yourself.

Cal Thomas is surely right. Our sin will find us out. But what is true for Spitzer is true for Thomas, and it is true for you and me. If we look a little deeper in the Bible, we find that we are all sinners, all guilty of something. It really doesn't take long to find something that we don't want exposed to the media, something that would make our spouses stand inches away but not touch us, something that would call into serious question our character and integrity.

Even if we aren't culpable physically of some certain sin, remember that God judges the heart and its wayward intentions. Jesus says anyone who has ever lusted is guilty of adultery. This is why the Bible says that no one is righteous and that all have sinned and fallen short of the glory of God. My guess is that most of us, unless we are soaked in denial and self-righteousness, see Spitzer exposed and humiliated and think, "Uh-oh, when is my number up?" Jesus says "judge not, that ye be not judged" for a reason.

Well, Jesus' number is up in this Palm Sunday reading. As we've said, he is being judged by Pilate, the chief priests, and the elders, who are worse than Wall Street and the media. The crime he's accused of is blasphemy, and the punishment is death.

And what is Jesus' response to the charges? What does he do? What does he say? *Nothing.* The Bible says, "But he gave him no answer, not even to a single charge." That's the "deafening sound," the sound of silence. Jesus doesn't defend himself, not even against a single charge.

What is your immediate response when you are accused of something? Who doesn't want to put up his dukes and fight? Who doesn't want to defend herself? Who doesn't want to launch a counter-attack? What husband out there, when accused about something by his wife, immediately says, "Thank you so very much, honey, for pointing out my deficiency! I'm so grateful to finally see the truth about myself"?

We try to be green in our house, so we wash our plastic Ziploc bags. We have bags older than our oldest child, who is almost 17. Since Christie does most of the cooking, I do much of the dishwashing. I hate washing the plastic bags. I'd throw them away, but I'm afraid that someone from Whole Foods or City Council might be watching me.

The other morning, when Christie came in and remarked that the pile of plastic bags in the sink was beginning to look like Mt. Everest, I naturally launched into a defensive and exhaustive account of all my household duties, which sadly took about four seconds. The fact that she does nearly everything to keep our house and children running didn't exactly enter into my thinking at that moment. I was more interested in describing the Herculean effort required to put a few plates in the dishwasher and press *Start*. Really, shouldn't I get a medal for that?

When you and I are accused of something, usually there is at least a kernel or a hint or a whiff of truth in the accusation. And even if the accusation is entirely wrong, then surely there is something else that we are guilty of that hasn't yet been brought to light. There is some flaw in our character or integrity that, if judged by the pure and good and true standards of God's Law would be indefensible, guilty as charged. There are no exceptions.

Except one. There was one who was righteous. There was one who was sinless. There was one who could defend with perfect immunity his own character and integrity. There was one who was always right and who was always loving. There was one who could defend himself against every charge. And standing before Pilate and the chief priests and the elders with his life at stake, "he gave no answer, not even to a single charge."

Who knows what was running through Jesus' mind at this moment of accusation? Maybe it was the Suffering Servant verses from Isaiah 53, verses that he would have known and identified with himself:

> He was oppressed, and he was afflicted,
>   yet he did not open his mouth;
> like a lamb that is led to the slaughter,
>   and like a sheep that before its shearers is silent,

so he did not open his mouth.

Why didn't Jesus defend himself? It's not right! It's not fair! Why didn't the one truly innocent person defend himself against the wicked charges of corrupt and guilty people? The answer, I think, is that Jesus refused to defend himself so that he could defend us.

Jesus is your defender. He doesn't defend himself, the righteous; he defends you, the unrighteous. If you know that tomorrow or later today you could be in front of cameras, accused of some sin, then Jesus is your defender. He will do more than stand inches from your side but not touch you. He will even do more than put his arm around you as you field the questions. What he will do for you is what you really long for him to do: He will take your place in the hot seat. He will field all the accusations thrown at you. He will be your substitute.

In our Prayers of the People, we say that Jesus is "our only Mediator and Advocate." That means that he is your defender, the defender of sinners. We have no need to defend ourselves! We would have no case before God if we did because there is no one who is righteous. "All we like sheep have gone astray; we have all turned to our own way." But the news of the Gospel is that we have been given one to defend us.

When accused and threatened with death on a cross, Jesus "never said a mumblin' word," as the spiritual says. He did not defend himself, for he knew that he must go to the cross to defend us. On the cross he absorbed the guilt, the judgment, the death that we deserved. As Jesus himself says, "God did not send the Son into the world to condemn the world, but in order that the world might be saved through him."

Today, whether you come in here bearing the guilt of the accused or the guilty pride of the accuser, there is one who has borne that guilt for you. Yes, it is true that, "All we like sheep have gone astray; we have all turned to our own way." But it is also true on this Palm Sunday, just as it is true and will be true on every day that dawns from now on to eternity, that "the LORD has laid on him the iniquity of us all."

Amen.

April 12, 2009 ‡ *Easter*

Only God Can Write Act V

JOHN 20:1-18

T here is an old dramatic truism: "Only God can write Act V." What this means is that the actors get themselves into such a pickle in the first four acts of the play that only God can come up with a resolution to the mess.

There is a preaching truism that is similar: never raise more snakes in the first part of your sermon than you can kill in the conclusion. We all know that there are plenty of snakes slithering through Acts I to IV. But today, Easter Day, is the day we celebrate Act V. And what an act! Only God can write Act V.

My hunch is that you've come here this morning needing an Act V. If your life is like mine, there are plenty of unresolved plot lines, unfortunate alliances, broken promises, premeditated betrayals, mixed motives, and loves lost that defy any hope of a happy ending. It may even seem to you that the Author of your life is intent on writing a tragedy, resolved only by death at the final curtain.

You may agree with Shakespeare, in *As You Like It*: "All the world's a stage, / And all the men and women merely players." If that is so, then what happens when we rifle through the allotment of our lives, what the playwright calls the seven ages of man: infant, schoolboy, lover, soldier, ... ? Well, according to the Bard, we reach the "[l]ast scene of all, / That ends this strange eventful history." Or, in Grateful Dead terms, "what a long, strange trip it's been."

But when we arrive at the final act of our lives, the end of the long, strange trip, is it true that we discover only a "second child-ishness and mere oblivion; / Sans teeth, sans eyes, sans taste, sans everything"? The modern, sound-bite version of Shakespeare's famous insight is "life's a pain, and then you die."

If any or all of this strikes you as true—if your life, along with its joys and routines, is peppered with strained or absent relation-ships, with circular patterns of destruction; if you find that you cannot rein in your anger or jealousy or greed or lust: in Bible lan-guage, your sin—then let me just tell you, you are in the right seat this Easter morning. Because today the curtain opens on Act V, the act only God can write.

As the curtain opens on Act V, what do we see? We see nothing at first, because the stage is dark. This is according to St. John's ac-count. We read that Easter Day, Act V, begins in the dark: "Early on the first day of the week, while it was still dark, Mary Magdalene came to the tomb." No one can see in the dark. Mary can't, either.

The day begins in blindness, but it does not end there. Easter Day ends, at least our account of it, in the light. Mary says to the disciples at the end of our reading, "I have *seen* the Lord." The day ends in sight.

What do the details of the account tell us about our own lives? What do we find in between the dark and the light, our infancy and final stage? We find, interestingly enough, much of the stuff that makes up Acts I to IV of our lives. Every good Act V includes some kind of reprisal of the play's previous acts.

In between the dark beginning and the bright ending, what do we see? Well, to start with, we see weeping. Mary breaks down cry-ing two times, sorrowing at her Lord's absence.

How often have you hoped to discover something and someone in your life, only to find nothing there? Any human life is in fact filled with heartbreak and disappointment. The right and human response is Mary's sorrow. As a wise Brahmin once said, "It is not a sign of good health to be well adjusted to a sick society." God gave us tear ducts for a reason!

What else do we see? Following typical gender lines, we see the men engaged in competition and rivalry. (I think if men cried, the world would be a more peaceful place!) Unlike Mary, who cries, Peter and John race to the tomb; John, the writer of the account, is quick to add that he arrives first. And I suppose, later, Peter obliged him to add that the chief apostle *enters* the tomb first, out of breath, but brave.

What else do we see in this account of Act V? We see rash and mistaken conclusions. Mary thinks she has understood the obvious facts on the ground. The tomb is empty; therefore Jesus' body must have been stolen. Through her veil of tears, Mary sees a man hanging around outside the empty grave, therefore the man must be the gardener.

How often do your read the facts on the ground in your life, only to jump to a wrong conclusion? He said this about me, therefore he must not like me. I've lost my job, therefore I have no worth. There is so much suffering in the world, therefore there is no God.

But just as our lives aren't a monolithic drumbeat of hurt, we see that sorrow, petty comparison, and wrongheaded conclusions are not all we find in this Gospel account of the first Easter. There are some more encouraging details as well.

We also see clues that are significant but puzzling; hopeful, but a little bewildering. John and Peter enter the tomb where their dead Lord had been wrapped and laid, only to find "the linen wrappings lying there, and the cloth that had been on Jesus' head, not lying with the linen wrappings but rolled up in a place by itself."

What linen cloth, what face cloth lies about your life, making you wonder? There is a phone call, a so-called 'coincidence,' a still small voice, an extraordinary confluence of events that can't help but have the thumbprint, even the faceprint of God on it. You may not be able to divine its actual or full meaning, but surely it's a clue meant to lead you onto the glorious conclusion that awaits you at the end of Act V.

We also see a kind of incomplete faith and partial understanding. John goes into the empty tomb, reads the clues and believes. His belief is incomplete, for as the text says, "as yet they did not understand the scripture." In a very real way, John's belief is our belief in this life. At its best, it is still partial and without comprehensive understanding. As Paul says, in this life, in Acts I to IV, we "see in a mirror, dimly."

Clues, incomplete faith, and partial understanding are not all we see, though. We also experience the presence of God! Angels, God's messengers, wait in the empty tomb and talk to Mary. Interestingly, Mary doesn't seem startled by this angelic conversation. Did she know that they were angels? Was she too consumed with her own grief to recognize the presence of God?

It makes me wonder how often in our lives, to use the language of Hebrews, we have "entertained angels unawares." How often have we been immersed in myopia, the naval gazing of our own lives, missing the wonder and presence of God right under our noses?

This may be so. And if Acts I to IV are all we're given, then the best we can hope for in this life is a mixture of sorrow, half-belief, and the so called "journey," with its clues and dead ends. To be honest, if that is all there is, then I would welcome the oblivion.

Thanks be to God we are given an Act V, the Act only God can write. We are not left on our own to recognize the presence of God. As we see, Mary sees Jesus himself and doesn't recognize him! So what happens? Jesus recognizes Mary! What this tells us is that Jesus Christ calls your name even in the midst of your incomplete belief, your mistaken identities, and your failure to recognize the presence of God.

At the center stage of Act V, we see Jesus Christ, standing beside an empty tomb, but not as a ghost or a phantom or a spirit. We see him with teeth, eyes, taste, everything. Death itself has been sent into oblivion. It is left lying powerless beside the discarded linen clothes. The tomb is all that is sans body, because Jesus is alive. Jesus is alive and talks directly to Mary—consoles her, cheers her, instructs her, calls her by name.

Today, this Easter Day, Jesus Christ is here. He is calling you by name: John, Catherine, Elizabeth, Paul. He knows your name and therefore knows your life. He is the author of your name and the author of your life. In him all the unresolved plot lines and mistaken identities, the missed chances and even the willful wrongdoing, are resolved. It is not a resolution that we can contrive or even conceive. But know this: it is better than you could ask for or imagine. Only God can write Act V.

Easter Day, like our lives, begins in the dark but ends in the light. For now we see in a mirror, dimly. But when we are raised as He has been raised, all will be clear. All of it will make sense. There will be no more weeping, no more sick society, no more mistaking, no more misunderstanding. There will be no need for clues, no more guesses at God's presence.

His presence will be all in all. There will be only Jesus Christ, at the very center, shining brighter than a thousand suns. And the best part is this: Act V will never, ever, ever end.

Amen.

April 18, 2007 ‡ *Wednesday after the Second Sunday of Easter (C)*

A Sermon for Virginia Tech

Two days prior, at Virginia Tech, a student opened fire at the school, killing 32 people and injuring 18 others before killing himself. This was among the deadliest mass shootings in American history.

I want to talk very briefly. This will be a very short sermon. Coming together to mourn with those who mourn, to pray for those who suffer, to affirm the truths of our faith, to confess our own sin, and to praise God in hymns in the midst of sorrow is what is needful. But I do think it is important to frame this terrible thing in the context of our Christian faith.

Many people have asked and are asking the question, "How could anybody do such a thing? I can't imagine how a person could perpetrate such violence. It doesn't make any sense." In fact, the headline in yesterday's paper was the quote "Senseless Shootings."

At first blush, this seems like a good and right question. Surely it is right to be appalled at the violence and death. But we are no different from the shooter. Every single one of us has the capability of doing exactly the same thing and even worse. I'm not just guessing about this. This is what Jesus says: "For out of the heart come evil intentions, murder, adultery, fornication, theft, false witness, slander."

Ultimately, better gun laws are not the solution, campus police aren't the problem, acculturation issues are not at fault. The problem lies within our hearts, each of our hearts.

Because each one of us—if the right set of pressures were applied, or some key ingredients in our so-called normal lives were taken away—could shoot down others and turn the gun on ourselves. The fact is that our lives are really a house of cards that can collapse at any time.

To see what happened at Virginia Tech in this way is to identify ourselves with Cho, the shooter. And to do this is to leave no room for judgment or self-righteousness. For as we read together from Psalm 130, *"If you, O LORD, should mark iniquities, / Lord, who could stand?"*

There is an ocean of grief and sorrow and anger, to be sure, along with a proper longing for justice. But to see within ourselves the same DNA as the killer, to accept Jesus' description of all of us, is to open the door to forgiveness and understanding and healing.

What I'm saying is that for the Christian who understands human nature, the killings make sense. Any of us could snap at any time.

It is important that what happened makes sense to us, but it is far more important that what happened makes sense to God. It makes sense to God because the main emotions in this awful thing are heartache and misery. It makes sense to God because God became a human who, as we read in Isaiah, was "despised and rejected of men; a man of sorrows, and acquainted with grief." He was a man who was "cut off out of the land of the living."

Our Lord suffered and suffers with those who suffer. Our Lord knows the depths of grief that a violent death causes. Like the students and professors who were killed on Monday, Jesus himself was cut off out of the land of the living. Grief and sorrow are familiar to him. To be killed mercilessly in the prime of life is what he himself experienced on the cross for our sake. Our iniquity he took upon himself, led like a lamb to the slaughter.

But our Lord who died is the Lord who did not stay dead. He rose again from the dead to give life to everyone who trusts in him. He gives life to those who reckon themselves among the murderers. He gives life to those who know that there is no health in them.

Life out of death really is the last word. That's why Jesus can tell his followers: "Do not let your hearts be troubled. Believe in God, believe also in me." In life and in death, God himself and God alone is our Rock and our Stronghold. He alone is not a house of cards. He alone is our protection. A Mighty Fortress is our God.

Amen.

May 18, 2014 ‡ *Fifth Sunday of Easter (A)*

I Will Not Show You The Way

JOHN 14:1-14

I n this morning's Gospel, Thomas asks a universal question: "How can we know the way?" There are many variations on the same theme, like "What am I supposed to do?" or "Where am I supposed to go from here?"

These are the kinds of questions that many are asking during this graduation season. They are also the questions we ask when we are in relationships that are failing and we see no way forward. *How can we know the way?*

These are the questions asked when careers are truncated or when they have stalled. *What am I supposed to do?* These are the questions we ask when our father is an alcoholic and keeps relapsing. These are the questions we ask when our adult child just cannot get it together and needs money again. *Where am I supposed to go from here?*

When you are in a place where these questions surface, the standard graduation answers just do not cut the mustard. 'Following your heart' or 'finding your passion' does not sufficiently address the level of your lostness or the depth of your need. What then are we to do? *How can we know the way?*

Writer Francis Spufford recounts his own "how can we know

the way" moment. He had been up all night fighting with his wife:

> We had been caught in one of those cyclical rows that re-ignite every time you think they've come to an exhausted close, because the thing that's wrong won't be left alone, won't stay out of sight if you try to turn away from it. ... Intimacy had turned toxic: we knew, as we went around and around and around in it, almost exactly what the other one was going to say, and even what they were going to think, and it only made things worse. ... When daylight came, the whole world seemed worn out.

I bet you've been there, too, in one way or another, even if you were just arguing with yourself!

The place to begin is not with the answer, but a few steps back. Thomas precedes his question with a confession of ignorance: "Lord, we do not know." Confessing that you do not know is a very good place to start when you are lost.

When Christie and I were first married, we spent our honeymoon backpacking through Europe. We decided to walk and hitchhike from the Italian country house we were staying in to Assisi. The distance was about 20 miles and crisscrossed farms and villages and major highways.

This was way before smart phones or GPS, and of course we were soon completely lost. The sane thing to do was to take out our Italian-English dictionary and ask somebody for directions. But, as we all know, men do not ask for directions; they know the way. Men do *not* not know the way. Men know the way, and they impress their young wives.

This man did not know the way, nor did he ask directions. Consequently, he did not impress his young wife. In fact, he got into a terrible, angry, sulking argument with his wife, even though it was his birthday, which made everything worse. We sure could have used the prayer of St. Francis then: "Lord, make me an instrument of your peace. When there is hatred, let me sow love; where there is injury, pardon." Maybe somebody was praying for us, because finally, hours and hours later, a kind nun stopped on the side of the road to pick us up and took us up the mountain to Assisi.

How can we know the way? It is a question that we ask all through life, and not just in marital arguments. It is a question you are asking this morning about some thing or person or absence in your life.

For those of us facing a fork in the road, how can we know the way? For those of at the end of the road, how can we know the way? For those of us at the beginning of the road, wondering where it will lead, how can we know the way? For those of us still on the same old road, worried that we just can't keep trudging along, how can we know the way? And for those of us completely off the road, just plain lost, how can we know the way?

Originally, the question is asked by Thomas and addressed to Jesus. Jesus answers him by saying, "I am the way." Last week Dave preached about Jesus' claim, earlier in John's Gospel, "I am the gate." Jesus claims to be not only the gate, the way that leads beyond the gate. I believe that what was true for Thomas then is true for you now. How can you know the way? Jesus says to you, "I am the way."

One thing that is important about Jesus' answer is what he does not say. He does not say, "I will show you the way." There is a big difference between "I am the way" and "I will show you the way." "I will show you the way" is like an impersonal set of directions. What you need to do with this relationship or life decision is x then y then z.

Maybe you know someone who always wants to show you the way. We had a distant relative, a very smart doctor, who would always take complicated life situations, boil them down to black and white, and tell you, "It's as simple as that: x, y, z." I always felt more lost after he showed me the way than I did before.

There are other problems with "I will show you the way." Maybe you perfectly understand the way you are being shown, but you lack the ability to follow it. Husbands, for example, are shown the way very clearly by Scripture. They are to love their wives as Christ loved the church. That means that they are to lay down their lives for their wives in each and every case. And yet, I don't know a single husband who does this perfectly. Maybe a few do it well. Most of us, me included, do it badly. Showing the way, knowing the way, is not the same as going the way. This is true in any number of situations:

loving your enemies, not worrying about tomorrow, refraining from envy.

One other problem with "I will show you the way" is that even when we are capable of going the way we are shown, sometimes we just don't want to. It's not that we lack the capacity but that we lack the will or the desire. Back to the prayer of St. Francis, I know it is better to console rather than seek consolation, but sometimes I just don't want to console; I want consolation.

Finally, you may have noticed that when someone shows you the way and you do not or cannot go the way they have shown, you begin to avoid that person. What may begin as so called 'good advice' from a person ends up being an impassable roadblock between you two, if you fail to follow the advice. This is why giving advice to anyone about anything is a dangerous and difficult enterprise. Not only do you not know all that is involved in another's situation, but you put your relationship in immediate jeopardy each time you say, "I will show you the way."

Thankfully, Jesus says to Thomas, as he says to you and me today, "I am the way." Another way to say this is that there is no way that Jesus is not, no road on which he is not on, no decision that he will not inhabit with you. There is a game show called *The Price is Right* on which a contestant had to choose Door #1, Door #2, or Door #3. The prize was only behind one door. "I am the way" means that Jesus is waiting for you behind Door #1, Door #2, *and* Door #3.

After all, Scripture says that nothing can separate us from the love of God in Christ Jesus—not even our lostness, our incapacity, or our unwillingness to go the way. No matter where we go, Jesus is the way. Are there any more comforting words than the psalmists?

> Where can I go from your spirit?
>   Or where can I flee from your presence?
> If I ascend to heaven, you are there;
>   if I make my bed in Sheol, you are there.
> If I take the wings of the morning
>   and settle at the farthest limits of the sea,
> even there your hand shall lead me,
>   and your right hand shall hold me fast.

I am the way. This is not to say that life's way does not include sorrow or difficulty, but it is to say that it does and always will include Jesus, the one who loves you, forgives you, and leads you—better yet, the one who holds you with his hand.

I'll close with Spufford's description of encountering the way when he could not see any way out. After his all-night argument, he went to a café "and nursed [his] misery along with a cappuccino." The barista put on a piece of music he knew and loved: Mozart's Clarinet Concerto, the middle movement, the adagio. He says,

> If you don't know it, it is a very patient piece of music. It too goes round and round, in its way, essentially playing the same tune again and again, on the clarinet alone and then with the orchestra, clarinet and then orchestra, lifting up the same unhurried lilt of solitary sound, and then backing it with a kind of messageless tenderness in deep waves, when the strings join in. ... It offers a strong, absolutely calm rejoicing, but it does not pretend there is no sorrow. On the contrary, it sounds as if it comes from a world where sorrow is perfectly ordinary, but there is still more to be said. I had heard it lots of times, but this time it felt to me like news. It said: everything you fear is true. And yet. And yet. Everything you have done wrong, you have really done wrong. And yet. And yet. ... [L]isten, and let yourself count, just a little bit, on a calm that you do not have to be able to make for yourself, because here it is, freely offered.

Amen.

May 9, 2010 ‡ *Sixth Sunday of Easter (C)*

Healing Begins with the Grace of God

JOHN 5:1-8

On the Monday prior, George Huguely, a Fourth Year at the University of Virginia, killed his ex-girlfriend, Yeardley Love. The murder made international headlines. Both were senior lacrosse players at UVA and were well-known to the Christ Church community.

L ast Tuesday, right after this terrible thing happened in and to our community, I got a call from George Huguely's defense attorney, asking if I might visit George in jail. We had gotten a call the day before from the jail; I was away and didn't get the call, so I gave my contact information to George in case it was he who called. I didn't know George or Yeardley personally but thought they might have come to our 5 pm service. And I knew for sure that many of our college students knew and loved both George and Yeardley.

That Tuesday afternoon, Christie and I were scheduled to meet with 15 or so girls from Yeardley's sorority and others who come to Christ Church. We were there to listen to and cry and pray with them. When I told the defense attorney this, she rightly asked, "Are you really able to minister to George *and* to all of Yeardley's friends?" She was right in asking this, just doing her job.

The answer to this question is what I want to talk about today. The answer is *yes*. The answer is yes because Christianity is the only narrative that has something true, something healing to say to both sides of this tragedy. If you're like me, you are weary of hearing about it. But there is something still to say this Sunday morning, because Christianity has a word of healing for both the victim and the perpetrator. The Gospel offers help for George and help for Yeardley. And the Gospel offers help for you, for at various times in your life you have been both the victim and the perpetrator.

First, in the reading from John, we find help for George and for all who have done any kind of wrong. We see an invalid, probably lame, paralyzed, or too sick or addicted to move. He's been that way for 38 years. He goes to the pool of Bethesda, a place that purportedly has healing properties. When the water is stirred, the first person into the water is healed. It stands to reason that, as the Bible says, many disabled people, "blind, lame, and paralyzed," lie there, waiting.

People gathered at this pool seeking healing and help. When you picture the scene, don't imagine a well-ordered hospital—UVA's, for instance—with clean halls and white gowns. Think instead of a makeshift medical outpost in Haiti for the crippled, deformed, and hopeless—a place where you find the blind, the lame, and the paralyzed.

I want to stop and make a connection here. Some of us have physical disorders and illnesses that put us in this man's camp, waiting by the pool. Or you have a child or a spouse or a parent who does. But all of us have suffered and are struggling with some form of blindness, lameness, or paralysis—maybe not for 38 years, but maybe so. Often it feels like forever, if you're suffering from depression, anxiety, or addiction. Or you just feel a deep sense of unworthiness that turns your world gray. Or you feel paralyzed with fear, anger, or lust. And in some ways, because of this thing, you feel like your life is on hold or out of control, while you lie on a mat, waiting for help that has not come.

Obviously, George is in this camp. You know the details of his life now, just like all of America. But don't think for a second that George is alone or somehow different. We are all in the same camp. The Gospel truth is that every single one of us is capable of doing what George did, or at least something like it. Every single one of us, if the right buttons were pushed, could find ourselves in handcuffs on a Monday morning.

After the Virginia Tech massacre, I preached this same message about Seung-Hui Cho, the gunman. Nobody really believed me because Cho was different. He was not like us. He had mental problems. He looked different. He was a monster. It was easy to demonize Cho because he was a so-called outsider.

When Christie and I were with the sorority girls on Tuesday, I asked them just to talk about their emotions. They felt anger at what happened to their friend. Their outrage was a fitting emotion, of course. But the girls' feelings were complicated because they knew and loved both Yeardley and George. George is not the outsider. He is, as Vice President Leonard Sandridge, said, "one of our own." George is not different, and he is not alone in his state. As Jesus says, out of every human heart comes all kinds of iniquity.

I say this not to be morbid but to remind us that we are bound together in our weakness. I love the story that my friend, who is now 100 years old, tells about her husband when he was a boy. One day he was walking down the street and he bumped into a woman who was cross-eyed. The woman said to him, "Young man, why don't you look where you're going!" To which the boy replied, "Ma'am, why don't you go where you are looking!" As Paul says, the thing I don't want to do is what I do, and the thing I want to do, I don't do. In one way or another, none of us really goes where he is looking. We constantly veer off the straight and narrow.

But off the straight and narrow, by the pool for invalids, is where Jesus comes into our lives. This is where you'll find him in your life. You won't turn to him otherwise. We don't get ourselves together and come to him. He comes to us as we're lying on our mats, paralyzed. Jesus comes to George in jail because George can't get out of jail to come to him. In your own jail, Jesus comes to you. He comes with forgiveness and healing.

When, in the Gospel reading, Jesus goes into this scene of despair and disease and spots the man lying on his mat, he asks him an important and not at all obvious question: "Do you want to be made well?" This is where many sermons on this passage go wrong. They pin the man's healing on his own willingness to be healed. "Show yourself worthy and willing, and God will heal you," they suggest. But when Jesus asks, "Do you want to be made well?" the man does *not* say yes. His response is ugly or at least flippant, something like, "You idiot, can't you see what's happening and has been happening for 38 years? Anyway, no one helps me."

Despite his impudence, Jesus comes to him on his mat and heals him. It's not because of his merit or his willingness or his desire. Jesus heals him not because the man is good but because God is good, because God is a God of grace and a God of healing. The man, having waited for 38 years, finally encounters grace. His healing begins with the grace of God.

On Tuesday, one girl asked, "What on earth could you say to George right now? What hope does he have for his life?" Because Jesus comes straight into our own messy lives with his grace and forgiveness and love, we do have something to say to George and to all of us: Jesus comes to you, loves you, forgives you. In him is your only hope of healing. He is a God of grace. When he comes to you on your mat and you feel and know his total love and acceptance of you in your illness, then your healing begins with the grace of God.

Of course, George will and should face the consequence of his actions. That is the law rightly at work. I pray it will be part of his healing, but healing usually involves some kind of pain and death. I want to use just one more example from *The Chronicles of Narnia*. It's the story of Eustace, a selfish boy who becomes so selfish that he turns into a dragon. In greed, he shoved a gold bracelet on his arm when he was still a boy; after he becomes a dragon the bracelet bites into his forearm causing great pain. He is miserable and is granted a change of heart—and unlike the man in our Gospel, we see that Eustace did have a desire to be healed.

Aslan the Lion comes into his scene of misery and leads him to a pool of water and tells him to undress. Eustace scratches off layers of dragon skin with his claws, but finds each layer knobbly and hard and tough. Finally, he gives up, but Aslan doesn't. Eustace recalls the experience this way:

> Then the lion said ... 'You will have to let me undress you.' I was afraid of his claws, I can tell you, but I was pretty nearly desperate now. So I just lay flat down on my back and let him do it.

The very first tear he made was so deep that I thought it had gone right into my heart. And when he began pulling the skin off, it hurt worse than anything I've ever felt. The only thing that made me able to bear it was just the pleasure of feeling the stuff peel off.

... Then he caught hold of me ... and threw me into the water. It smarted like anything but only for a moment. After that it became perfectly delicious and ... all the pain had gone from my arm. And then I saw why. I'd turned into a boy again.

The healing begun by the grace of God always involves pain because it always leads to death, the death of *self*—the death of the very thing that is killing you. It is the thing you've tried to scratch away by yourself without success, the thing that Jesus must take away for you.

George and his family are experiencing a kind of death that I pray will lead to healing through this word of grace. Yeardley and her family of course have experienced a literal death, which I trust will lead to a deeper and permanent healing through the Gospel, too. Here we have help not just for Yeardley, but for everyone. As Dave said in his sermon last week, we do not know when our own appointment with death will be. I've done four funerals in the last four weeks; mine could be the fifth.

The help for Yeardley is the same for all who have died in Christ, that she has gone to a place where, as we read in Revelation, there is no night. The night, with all it's darkness and all its terror, the one particular night of a week ago, does not exist there. There is no night there.

But there is "the river of the water of life," which will wash away all scent of hurt and trauma, all memory of pain and loss. And there is "the tree of life," whose leaves are "for the healing of the nations"—and that includes our cities, our communities, our families, especially two of them right now. Those leaves are for the healing of a young woman who is now made perfect, and they are for a young man, whose healing, like everyone's healing, must begin with the grace of God.

Amen.

May 17, 2015 ‡ *Seventh Sunday of Easter (B)*

A Commencement for Outcasts

JOHN 17:6-19

O ur Gospel passage from John seems to serendipitously fall in the liturgical year right around graduation time. Jesus is transitioning, too. Thursday was Ascension Day, the day the resurrected Jesus leaves his disciples and returns to his heavenly Father. Our passage today constitutes a kind of commencement address, Jesus' words to his 'students' before they go out on their own.

You can easily hear plenty of canned graduation pablum, so I thought I would give you a few good, light-hearted quotes from commencement addresses of the past. You heard a good one from Mr. Rogers in Willis' sermon last week, and here are some more.

Bill Watterson, of *Calvin and Hobbes* fame, in 1990: "What's it like in the real world? Well, the food is better, but beyond that I don't recommend it." Dolly Parton in 2009: "Now I usually try not to give advice—information, yes; advice, no. But what has worked for me might not work for you. Well, take for instance: What has worked for me? Wigs, tight clothes, push-up bras, high-heel shoes ..."

And a zinger from FDR in 1932, reminding us of how things never really change: "As you have viewed the world of which you are about to become a more active part, I have no doubt that you have been impressed by its chaos."

Because the world still impresses us with it's chaos, we thankfully have Jesus' words from circa AD 30. Jesus' commencement address is in the form of a prayer. Talking about his disciples, he says to the Father, "And now I am no longer in the world, but they are in the world, and I am coming to you." What then does Jesus say we need in this world of chaos? He prays, "Holy Father, protect them." We need protection.

Why would we need protection in this world? The ancient renunciations in our baptismal liturgy this morning remind us of the triumvirate of forces aligned against us, from the cosmological to the personal. First there is "Satan and all the spiritual forces of wickedness that rebel against God." Next there are "the evil powers of this world which corrupt and destroy the creatures of God." And finally, there are our own "sinful desires that draw [us] from the love of God."

This view of the world does not mean that the world wasn't created good, or that truth and beauty and love don't exist in the world. Louis Armstrong's "What a Wonderful World" always makes me cry: "I see skies of blue, clouds of white, / The bright blessed day, the dark sacred night, / And I think to myself, What a wonderful world." This was played at a recent wedding reception, where the world was wonderful indeed. The bride and groom both exuberant with joy, the late evening sun on the green hills of Albemarle County, with food, drink, friends, and love all around. It was one of those times when you think to yourself, *What a wonderful world—thanks be to God.* You've had moments like this. I hope you have a lot of them.

I think I cry at that song because I'm grateful when it rings true in experience, and I'm also longing for the day when Jesus comes back to make all things new, to make the world wonderful for everybody all the time. Because, obviously, the world is not wonderful all the time.

There are earthquakes, murder trials, train wrecks, and miscarried babies. There is bigotry and injustice, inequity and scarcity. There is betrayal, self-righteousness, and narcissism. Sometimes we do see "friends shaking hands, saying, 'How do you do?' / They're really saying, 'I love you,'" but other times our sinful hearts are really saying "I envy you, I lust after you, or I want to be rid of you."

Because this world impresses us with its chaos, we need protection. And protection is what Jesus prays for because he even says that the world hates his followers just as it hated him. He says that we are not to be taken out of the world but to be protected in it. This means there is no flight from the world or its problems; even if you are a hermit, you still have to deal with all the sinful desires that draw you from the love of God.

In the novel *The French Lieutenant's Woman* by John Fowles, we meet a woman who suffers in this world, a woman in need of protection. Being in Victorian England, she is a 'fallen' woman, ridiculed, judged, and derided by her small community. She is an outcast.

She shares her tragedy with a man she feels she can trust. He responds, "But my dear Miss Woodruff, if every woman who'd been deceived by some unscrupulous member of my sex were to behave as you have—I fear the country would be full of outcasts." Miss Woodruff answers, "It is. ... Outcasts who are afraid to seem so."

"Outcasts," or "outcasts who are afraid to seem so," seems to me an apt description of how many or even most people feel in this world. An outcast doesn't really belong. We are, in fact, all outcasts, as we are the spiritual descendants of Adam and Eve who were cast out of the Garden of Eden, the original wonderful world. Maybe that is why Jesus says in his commencement prayer that we "do not belong to this world."

What does an outcast need? An outcast needs to belong somewhere. An outcast needs to be taken in somewhere. An outcast needs someone else's protection from the world, the flesh, and the devil. That protection comes, I think, in the form of Jesus' second request in his commencement prayer: He prays that we would be sanctified. To be sanctified just means to be set apart, singled out by God himself.

This set-apartness is most powerfully illustrated in our baptismal liturgy. Babies are vulnerable and helpless. Every parent I know prays for protection for his or her children. Having recognized and renounced the evil of the world, we turn to Jesus Christ as savior and put our whole trust in his grace and love. He takes us in and protects us with the indissoluble bond of baptism.

The mark of the cross in oil on a baby's forehead sanctifies, sets apart, this child: "you are sealed by the Holy Spirit in Baptism and marked as Christ's own forever." Talk about protection. After his baptism a few months ago, a 4-year-old boy asked his mother on the way home, "When the oil from the cross on my head wears off, does that mean I'm not baptized anymore?" Of course the cross is there forever, a symbol of our heavenly Father's protective hand. We who were cast out of the Garden of Eden into the dangerous world are brought in forever.

All this is because Jesus, who prays this prayer of protection for us, became an outcast himself. He could have called for the protection of angels when the world, the flesh, and the devil conspired against Him. But for our sake, and for the sake of this wonderful world, he gave himself up to death on the cross.

I'll close with the final scene from the Georges Bernanos novel, *The Diary of a Country Priest*. A sickly young priest is in his first parish out of seminary. He is rejected by his people and sees himself as a failure. His stomach pains increase through the book. At one point he stays up all night to pray but is unsuccessful. He finally concludes, "God had withdrawn Himself from me—of this at any rate I am sure." Certainly, a feeling most of us can relate to.

The priest is finally diagnosed with stomach cancer. He dies in the derelict home of an unbelieving friend who dropped out of seminary. The friend tries to arrange for the local priest to bring the sacrament to the dying man, but he doesn't arrive in time, and the young priest dies. The friend recalls his final moments:

> The priest was still on his way, and finally I was bound to voice my deep regret that such delay threatened to deprive my comrade of the final consolations of our Church. He did not seem to hear me. But a few moments later he put his hand over mine, and his eyes entreated me to draw closer to him. He then uttered these words almost in my ear. ...
>
> 'Does it matter? Grace is ... everywhere.'
>
> I think he died just then.

And that is the commencement for outcasts: Grace is everywhere.

Amen.

June 1, 2014 ‡ *Seventh Sunday of Easter (A)*

Casting Lessons

1 PETER 5:6-11

T here is a gem of a verse tucked into our 1 Peter reading this morning. It is a Scripture so full of comfort and promise that we have it on our welcome page on our website. Quite simply and directly, Peter says, "Cast all your anxiety on him, because he cares for you." What does this mean for us? How can it be a word of comfort for us this morning?

Let's start with the word "anxiety." It is alternatively translated as "cares" or "worries." This is one word that does not require the preacher to expend much effort to explicate or elucidate. I suspect that your cares and anxieties are very much front and center, as are mine. Sometimes, you find that worries, like the sorrows Claudius describes in Hamlet, "come not single spies / But in battalions." This is why the sleeping pill was invented.

Not a single person I know really likes waking up worried in the middle of the night or dealing with vague anxiety during the day. Worried people would like to change their states of mind. There is a funny *New Yorker* cartoon in the recent edition of the magazine. A caterpillar comes into a therapist's office in need of help. He is lying on the couch. The therapist happens to be a big butterfly. She is standing up on her therapist's chair, towering over the caterpillar, gesticulating with her many legs, saying, "The thing is, you really have to *want* to change."

Assuming we want to change anxiety into peace, the text today opens for us a way forward. And for that we look at the word "cast": "Cast all your anxiety on him." "Cast" is also translated as "put" or "give" or "throw" or "turn" all your anxiety over to him. Each verb suggests action on our part.

When I hear the word "cast," I immediately think of fly fishing. This can actually increase rather than reduce anxiety, as my cast is always in need of serious improvement. There are times on the river, especially when the trout are easily spooked, when your cast has to be absolutely perfect in order to catch the fish. There can be no drag in the line. The fly must be presented to the fish in the most natural way.

Casting a fly rod is no easy task, not for me anyway. I get excited by the fish's rise and hurry the backcast. I try to muscle the line through the wind, instead of letting the rod tip release it with power. Sometimes, fly-fishing, which is supposed to provide a zen-like release from worry, becomes yet another occasion for anxiety, especially when my partners are landing fish while I am untangling yet another wind knot. I need casting lessons.

In the same way, many of us have quite a bit of difficulty casting our cares on God. Or we may cast them but then immediately reel them back in. Or we may find that we really have no idea how to cast our cares on God to begin with. We need casting lessons.

Norman Maclean makes this connection at the beginning of *A River Runs Through It*. "In our family," he says, "there was no clear line between religion and fly fishing." The narrator's father is a Presbyterian minister who spends as many hours a week teaching his boys to cast as he does teaching the catechism. The casting instructions, more than the catechism, taught the true nature of man's fallen state:

> if you have never picked up a fly rod before, you will soon find it factually and theologically true that man by nature is a damn mess. ...
>
> Well, until man is redeemed he will always take a fly rod too far back, just as natural man always overswings with an

ax or golf club and loses all his power somewhere in the air; only with a rod it's worse, because the fly often comes so far back it gets caught behind in a bush or rock. ...

Then, since it is natural for man to try to attain power without recovering grace, he whips the line back and forth making it whistle each way, and sometimes even snapping off the fly from the leader, but the power that was going to transport the little fly across the river somehow gets diverted into building a bird's nest of line, leader, and fly that falls out of the air into the water about ten feet in front of the fisherman.

Perhaps we cannot and do not naturally cast our anxiety on God because, as Maclean says, not only are we a damn mess, but we want to attain and keep power without recovering grace. The connection between control and anxiety is an obvious one. Sometimes we clutch our cares so tightly in our fists that we cannot even begin to cast them on God.

Fortunately for us, God is at work notwithstanding our ability or inability to cast our cares on him. Why? As the verse says, "because he cares for you." That's the third word to examine this morning: "care." God's care is like the care of a mother for her newborn infant. The infant can't cast its worries away. Its mother just takes her infant and meets every need, every care, with love and completeness. God cares for us in this way, *especially* when we cannot let go of our anxieties, however much we may want to.

Will McDavid's commentary on Genesis, *Eden and Afterward*, underscores the difficulty of "letting go," as well as God's care for us on our behalf. As he writes, God "will be at work regardless of whether we 'let' him by backing off. 'Let go and let God,' the popular saying, is bad theology insofar as it implies he will not work unless we let him. God's operations are his prerogative."

Think back to the caterpillar on the therapist's couch. Yes, wanting to change, even doing all we can to cast our cares on him because he cares for us, is a good and right thing. Often we experience incredible peace by placing our cares at the foot of the cross. Yet the caterpillar is created and bound by a force much greater than his own nature or his wants. Whether he wants to or not, he will turn into a butterfly. In due time, he will fly gently off into the summer air, arrayed in brilliant colors, lighting on a green leaf. A power greater than his worries is at work. That is the ultimate casting lesson.

This is what Peter means when he says a few verses later, that "after you have suffered a little while, the God of all grace, who has called you to his eternal glory in Christ, will himself restore, support, strengthen and establish you." *Restore, support, strengthen, and establish*—that's what God means by "care." And as a rejoinder to the natural man who attempts to attain power without recovering grace, Peter ends the passage, "To him be power forever and ever. Amen."

You are probably aware that the poet Maya Angelou died last week. She was well acquainted with anxieties and cares and worries, as she was a childhood victim of rape who was raised in poverty and suffered through segregation. She had a keen sense of the human heart and a profound ability to speak directly to the heart. She once said, "The desire to reach for the stars is ambitious. The desire to reach hearts is wise." She was a wise woman.

Ms. Angelou was also well acquainted with the God of the Bible, the God who says, "Cast all your anxiety on me, because I care for you." In 1993, Christie and I had the privilege of attending Bill Clinton's inauguration. We were in Alexandria for seminary and went with the masses to the National Mall. We heard Ms. Angelou recite what has become her most famous poem, "On the Pulse of Morning."

I'll close with an excerpt from that poem. Throughout the poem, the Rock and the River, both capital Rs, are the obvious voices of God, asking you for your cares and worries and anxieties. You don't need them, and he can and does and will take them on himself:

> Across the wall of the world,
> A River sings a beautiful song. It says,
> Come, rest here by my side.

Amen.

June 9, 2019 ‡ *Pentecost (C)*

I Can't Get No Satisfaction

JOHN 14:8-17, 25-27

I came across a funny cartoon last week. The first frame was "God as Dog," with a friendly dog looking out loyally at the viewer. The caption said, "I will always be with you." The second frame was "God as Cat," with a mercurial looking cat lounging regally. The caption said, "Depart from me!"

We've got the "God as Dog" variety this morning on Pentecost Sunday. Jesus tells his disciples that the Father will send them the Holy Spirit who will "be with you forever." In Acts, we see that this Spirit comes to the disciples with rushing wind and tongues of fire when they are gathered together in Jerusalem after Jesus' death, resurrection, and ascension. The Spirit enables them to praise God in diverse and foreign tongues. The Spirit emboldens them to preach, teach, heal, and spread the Gospel throughout the world.

That same Holy Spirit is still present today, empowering people to do all those same things. But the account of Pentecost in Jerusalem may seem removed from most people's experience, so I want to focus on Philip's request to Jesus this morning: He wants God to be with us. You and I seem to share that longing, otherwise we wouldn't be here in church this morning. We want God to be with us, which is another way of saying that we want to know God.

Philip says to Jesus, "Lord, show us the Father, and we will be satisfied." Jesus responds with a question: "Have I been with you all this time, Philip, and you still do not know me? Whoever has seen me has seen the Father. How can you say, 'Show us the Father'? Do you not believe that I am in the Father and the Father is in me?" What are we to make of that interchange?

The first point is important but well-trodden, so I won't belabor it. It's that we will never be satisfied as human beings without knowing God. "Our heart is restless until it rests in Thee," St. Augustine wrote. The obvious charms of the world—money, power, fame, sex—famously fail to satisfy, even though most people still cast their nets into these waters. But Mick Jagger was right: "I try and I try and I try and I try / I can't get no satisfaction."

What is less obvious is that even good works and a life of service will not finally satisfy us either. There was an interesting article in the *New York Times* last week about a group of Millennials who moved into a convent with some catholic nuns. The project is called "Nuns and Nones," the N-O-N-E variety being a burgeoning demographic of people with no religious affiliation. The article begins:

> Sarah Jane Bradley was an unmarried, 'spiritual but not religious' professional in her early 30s, with a rowdy group of friends and a start-up when she moved out of her communal house and into a convent.
> A bunch of friends went with her.
> They called the project Nuns and Nones, and they were the "nones"—progressive millennials, none of whom were practicing Roman Catholics. Intended to be a pilot project, the unusual roommate situation with the Sisters of Mercy would last for six months.

These millennials had committed themselves to work for social justice and wanted to learn from the nuns, who worked with sick and the homeless. Admirable, for sure, and an interesting experiment. However,

> The sisters began to see that the millennials wanted a road map for life and ritual, rather than a belief system. On one

of the first nights, Sister Judy Carle said, one of the young people casually asked the sisters, 'So, what's your spiritual practice?'

'That's the first question, not, "What do you believe?"'

The Bible, both the Old and New Testaments, clearly teaches that even a life of good works or spiritual practices will not satisfy our deepest human desires. Only relationship with God, knowing God, will satisfy. This is why Philip says, "Lord, show us the Father, and we will be satisfied."

The Bible also teaches us that relationship with God is neither spiritual nor religious. Relationship with God is *personal*. I would argue that all those who self-identify as 'spiritual but not religious' are looking for the same thing as the rest of us—personal relationship with God. Jesus' response to Philip tells us this: "Have I been with you all this time, Philip, and you still do not know me?" In other words, there is a big difference in knowing about God and knowing God.

This hits home for church people, especially liturgical church people. We may know the church season colors, we may volunteer at the soup kitchen, we may have memorized portions of the Book of Common Prayer, but if we do not know God personally, we will not be satisfied. The more evangelical wing of the Church has been right to talk about our "personal relationship with the Lord," and accepting Jesus as our "personal Savior." The language might be trite now, but the essence of it is true.

We also may think we know God, but maybe we are mistaken. Sometimes we think we know something or somebody when we really don't. I had a very funny experience at a graduation party a few weeks ago. A man introduced me to his wife, whose work overlaps with many Christ Church parishioners. She cut her husband off and said to me, "Oh, I know who you are. You should know that people love you." I responded with some kind of humblebrag, like, "You can only fool them for so long," but of course I was eating up the positive affirmation.

Then she put her hand on my arm and said, "I mean, people really love you. After they say your name, they feel so much emotion, they have to pause." Then, as a demonstration of this, *she said an-*

other minister's name! She had mistaken me for the pastor of another church in town! Her husband said, "Um, honey, he's not him. This is Paul Walker," to which she said, "Oh," then walked away to refill her wine glass.

As I said, there is a big difference in knowing about God and knowing God personally. This, again, is illustrated by Jesus' response to Philip. Philip says that he wants to see the Father, and then he'll be satisfied. Jesus says whoever has seen him has seen the Father. There are two different Greek words here that mean "see." Philip uses the word that means simply "to look at with your eyes." But Jesus responds with a word that means "to understand with your heart." We use the word "see" to mean both those things. We see another person in front of us. But when we really understand who they are, we say, "Oh, now I see."

There is deep satisfaction in seeing and knowing a particular subject, like a certain period of history, or the ecosystem of a specific habitat. There is a deeper satisfaction in seeing and knowing another person, being in honest, intimate relationship. And there is the deepest satisfaction in knowing and being known by God. If we want to know God, then Jesus tells us that he is the way.

Even liturgical church people like us long for personal relationship with God. The question for parents and godparents in our baptismal liturgy is the question for us all: "Do you turn to Jesus Christ and accept him as your Savior?" To see him on the cross, dying for your sins, is to see and know that he will always be with you. That is good news. The even better news is that even if you do not yet know him, you can be sure that he knows you.

Amen.

May 26, 2013 ‡ *Trinity Sunday (C)*

The Gospel According to Quasimodo

ROMANS 5:1-5

I n *The Hunchback of Notre-Dame*, Victor Hugo explains the existence of sanctuaries:

> Every city during the Middle Ages ... had its places of asylum. These sanctuaries, in the midst of the deluge of penal and barbarous jurisdictions which inundated the city, were a species of islands which rose above the level of human justice. Every criminal who landed there was safe. ...
>
> His foot once within the asylum, the criminal was sacred; but he must beware of leaving it; one step outside the sanctuary, and he fell back into the flood.

You might remember the plot line of the novel. (I would add a spoiler alert to this sermon, but you have had 183 years to read the book!) Quasimodo is the hideously deformed bell ringer in the Notre-Dame Cathedral. His master is an archdeacon who presides over the cathedral, a cruel man who becomes obsessed with a beautiful gypsy girl named La Esmeralda. The archdeacon stalks the girl, who is in love with a handsome but shallow military captain. One night the captain arranges a tryst with the girl and the creepy archdeacon follows them to an inn and watches them from an adjoining room. (Pretty racy for 1831.)

When the moment comes to its climax, so to speak, the obsessed archdeacon busts into the room and plunges a knife into the captain's heart. He escapes through a window, leaving the captain in a pool of blood on the floor and La Esmeralda framed and arrested for murder.

The archdeacon, who believes he is in love with the girl, stands by in silence as the girl is tried, tortured, and convicted. La Esmeralda is sentenced to death by hanging. On the morning of her execution, Quasimodo spies her approaching the gallows from his perch by the cathedral bells. He races down and snatches her away, even as the rope is encircling her neck. The hunchback carries her across the threshold of Notre-Dame, bringing her to a place of safety and sanctuary.

The place of sanctuary or safety from condemnation is a powerful image. Who doesn't desire to be carried across some kind of threshold into a place where you are totally immune from "barbarous jurisdictions" of any kind, whatever form your kind may take. In Hugo's novel, the girl is accused by a corrupt legal system, but the responsible party is the one who embodies the religious law.

The archdeacon is an earlier and more sinister version of the character Javert in *Les Mis*, relentlessly pursuing the escaped convict Jean Valjean. In both novels, Hugo says the purpose of the law, whether holy or corrupt, is to chase down and convict you.

Being carried into a place of sanctuary, a place immune from the law is an apt metaphor for St. Paul's description of Law and grace in his epistle to the Romans. In the first part of the letter he argues that everyone, both Jew and Gentile alike, is guilty of transgressing the law. After the universal conviction, he announces the sentence: death. "For the wages of sin is death," he says a little later on.

In today's lesson, Paul begins with the way that we are carried across the threshold into sanctuary, and that is justification by faith: "Therefore, since we are justified by faith, we have peace with God through our Lord Jesus Christ, through whom we have obtained access to this grace in which we stand." As Hugo says of sanctuary, "His foot once within the asylum, the criminal was sacred." When the blameworthy are justified by faith, they become blameless.

I've noticed that for many modern people, the concept of individual, not to mention universal, guilt under God's law is suspect at best and noxious at worst. In some cases, this may be a subconscious corrective to legalistic, fire-and-brimstone preaching that has sadly passed for Christianity, much like the archdeacon's character.

But its absence may also have to do with the steady diet of "you're a good person and nothing you do could possibly be wrong as long as you believe in yourself and try your best" that everyone who ever watched any show on television has been fed. One problem with this diet is that it gives us an unrealistic view of ourselves.

An article in the *Scientific American* addressed a popular Dove commercial. Women are asked to describe their faces to sketch artists who draw their portraits. These same women have also had their faces described to the artist by strangers with whom they've just interacted. The women discover that the stranger's description leads to a more beautiful picture of themselves. The ad ends, "You're more beautiful than you think."

As it turns out, that's just not true: "The evidence from psychological research," some of which was done here at the University of Virginia,

> suggests instead that we tend to think of our appearance in ways that are more flattering than are warranted. This seems to be part of a broader human tendency to see ourselves through rose colored glasses. Most of us think that we are better than we actually are—not just physically, but in every way.

The problem with "adaptive self-enhancement," as it's called, quite apart from its inaccurate biblical anthropology, is that it doesn't leave much room for dealing with places of actual guilt and wrongdoing that everyone experiences. This is also true for certain religious narratives that expect that once you're saved you will continue to improve in an upward ascent into holiness.

In those narratives, you have no category in which to place your churning lust or subtle dishonesty or consuming ambition. You have no place to register your failure. What happens when, despite your best effort, your marriage fails? How do you understand the relationships that have iced over? What do you do with your inability to stop certain behaviors or self-destructive ideations? Despite the axiom, clearly it's not "all good."

When it's not "all good," adaptive self-enhancement isn't enough. It's never enough to quiet the inner or outer voices of judgment that flood us no matter what picture of ourselves we draw. We need to be carried into a place of sanctuary, where those voices cannot reach us, where we're safe from the flood.

Thankfully, we do not have to be justified by self, since we are justified by faith. We have obtained access to the sanctuary we need. As Paul says later, "There is therefore now no condemnation for those who are in Christ Jesus."

I wonder if Hugo, when thinking about Quasimodo, had these words from Isaiah in mind:

> he had no form or majesty that we should look at him,
>   nothing in his appearance that we should desire him.
> He was despised and rejected by others;
>   a man of suffering and acquainted with infirmity;
> and as one from whom others hide their faces
>   he was despised, and we held him of no account.

We are justified not by a general faith but by faith in a specific person, the one whom Isaiah foretells. We too have been carried across the threshold by our Lord Jesus Christ, just as Quasimodo carried the condemned girl into the safe space of Notre-Dame. The grace in which we stand gives us immunity from the Law.

Though we are immune from condemnation, we still suffer its effects. Paul says the final effect of the Law and sin is death. Obviously, we are not immune from death. But here the Gospel according to Quasimodo reaches even into death. Through no fault of her own, La Esmeralda leaves the place of sanctuary. She's captured and eventually hanged. Quasimodo is broken by grief and disappears.

The only sign of him is discovered years later in a forsaken tomb. Two skeletons are entwined in an embrace; one who had been hanged, and one with a twisted spine and head sunk down between its shoulders. The latter had not been hanged; he had just come there and died. This is the Gospel according to Quasimodo: Even in death, we are embraced by Jesus Christ. For if we have died with him, we will be raised with him. He who carries us into sanctuary will carry us all the way.

Amen.

June 1, 2008 ‡ *Third Sunday after Pentecost*

By Faith and Not By Sight

GENESIS 6:9-22, 7:24, 8:14-19

I recently reread Harper Lee's *To Kill A Mockingbird*. It's one of my all-time favorite novels. Everyone loves this book: she won a Pulitzer Prize and was awarded three honorary degrees for her work. *To Kill A Mockingbird* is so nearly perfect that it is easy to see why Lee never wrote another novel. How could you follow up on something so good?

And yet, as she was writing the novel, Harper Lee was so frustrated with her efforts that after her third full revision she threw the entire manuscript out of her New York window. She was determined to leave it on the streets until her editor convinced her to reclaim it and submit it. The rest is southern literature history.

I love this story because it is so easy to relate to Lee's emotion. Who hasn't wanted to take something you've been working on and throw it out the window? Just be done with the whole thing. Children working on a drawing will get frustrated and rip the paper out of the notebook and ball it up and throw it away. Or if a toy is broken, if it won't work right, the toy gets hurled across the room.

The scary part is that this emotion runs deeper than a children's drawing, or even a Pulitzer Prize winning novel. We get frustrated by what is broken in our lives, and the temptation is to throw it out the window. This includes jobs. Do you remember "Take This Job and Shove It"? Number one on the country music hits list in 1978.

More tragically, the out-of-the-window mentality includes people. Broken marriages are thrown away. Broken children get sent away. Broken elderly parents get put away.

Hemingway said, "The world breaks everyone." And broken people break themselves in ways that range from mundane to suicidal.

There is no judgment here. I'm right there with you. Sometimes the problems are just too complex; sometimes the relationships are too painful and broken; sometimes the brokenness of the world is just too much to handle. You just want to wipe it all away and be done with it.

This is exactly what happens in our reading from Genesis this morning. We read about Noah and his ark and his animals, two by two. It is such a funny thing that Noah's ark is generally thought of as a children's story. At our house, we've got several different versions of it, not to mention little toy arks with giraffes and monkeys and zebras. The animals are nice, and the big boat is really interesting, but the story itself is terrifying. God decides to wipe us all away and be done with us.

In Genesis 6 we read,

> The LORD saw that the wickedness of humankind was great in the earth, and that every inclination of the thoughts of their hearts was only evil continually. And the LORD was sorry that he had made humankind on the earth, and it grieved him to his heart. So the LORD said, "I will blot out from the earth the human beings I have created—people together with animals and creeping things and birds of the air, for I am sorry that I have made them.

The Lord took all of his creation and threw it out of the window.

Although we read that the Lord chose Noah to be the agent of redemption for creation, it is easy to still feel that God has given up on his creation. Yes, after the flood God promises not to bring this kind of destruction upon the earth again, and he sets the rainbow in the sky as a sign of his covenant. But when you look at current events, the devastation in Myanmar, for example, and the rising death toll from the earthquake in China, you can be forgiven for wondering whether the Lord has forgotten his promise. When you look at the world food crisis and the starvation facing Ethiopian children, one can be forgiven for wondering whether the rainbow means anything at all. When you look at how fundamentally broken the world is, then one can be forgiven for wondering whether God has given up on the world.

Another version of the question "Has God given up on the world?" is "Has God given up on *me*?" Although you may think that the description "every inclination of the thoughts of your heart is only evil continually" is a little strong, you may still relate to the Bible's assessment of your human condition.

The headlines in the paper last week labeled an accused man as a "recidivist," meaning he keeps doing the same thing. We're all recidivist when it comes to sin, aren't we? How many times do you have to say sorry for the same transgression? Parents like to say, "Young man! How many times must I tell you the same thing? Haven't you learned your lesson yet?" On one level all of humanity says, "No, we haven't learned our lesson, because we still fall into sin. Or perhaps we have learned our lesson, but it has no power to keep us on the straight and narrow."

This is the struggle the poet John Donne wrestles with in his poem "A Hymn to God the Father":

> Wilt thou forgive that sin which I have won
> Others to sin, and made my sin their door?
> Wilt thou forgive that sin which I did shun
> A year or two, but wallow'd in, a score?
> When Thou hast done, thou hast not done,
> For I have more.

Has God given up on the world? Has God given up on me? This kind of despair in the face of the hurt and brokenness of the world isn't an 'unchristian' response. It is a human response, a response of sadness in the face of hurt and sorrow, a response to the facts on the ground. I think it's an important response for any thinking, feeling, wondering person.

And yet this morning's reading from Genesis allows another response as well, a response of faith. Even though the facts on the ground appear one way, the facts of faith appear another. We read that God hasn't given up on us. The floods came, but they receded. Dry ground emerged. Noah and his family stepped off the boat into the sunshine.

The Bible says that "we walk by faith, not by sight." Walking by faith and not by sight leads us to the same conclusion as Longfellow:

> And in despair I bowed my head;
> 'There is no peace on earth,' I said;
>   'For hate is strong,
>   And mocks the song
> Of peace on earth, good-will to men!'
> Then pealed the bells more loud and deep:
> 'God is not dead, nor doth He sleep;
>   The Wrong shall fail,
>   The Right prevail,
> With peace on earth, good-will to men.'

Although we cannot skip over the devastation in the Noah account, we also cannot ignore the saving love of God for his creation. We cannot ignore his promise, signified in the rainbow, to make "The Right prevail." God has not given up on his world.

And God has not given up on you. Even though you may feel like you are trying his patience, God has not given up on you. Our preacher friend Tim Keller tells the story of his struggle as a recidivist. He knew that Jesus was his savior and advocate, but he still struggled with the same sin over and over again. Then he would imagine a scenario in which Jesus would go before the Father and say, "Um, sorry, but it's about Tim again. Yes, I know we had this same conversation last week."

Do you ever feel like this? Keller finally came to the Gospel conclusion that this is not how that scene plays out at all. Because, he says, "God doesn't seek the same payment twice." God doesn't seek the same payment twice.

What Keller means is what the Bible means in its assurance that God hasn't given up on you or the world. Yes, we say that because we walk by faith and not by sight. But, we don't walk by blind or unproven faith. God substantiated his promise. First, he sent a rainbow, but in the fullness of time he sent his Son. Yes, Noah was obedient to God and so the world was saved for the moment through an ark. But ultimately Jesus was obedient to God and the world was saved forever through a cross.

God doesn't seek the same payment twice. We know that Jesus once and for all made payment for the brokenness of the world. We know that Jesus once and for all made payment for the sin you've wallowed in over and over. The world will break you, yes, and you are broken. But God arranged for the world to break Jesus, so that by his stripes we are healed.

God has not thrown you or his world out of the window. He will not wipe you away and be done with you. "I am confident of this, that the one who began a good work among you will bring it to completion by the day of Jesus Christ."

Amen.

July 4, 2010 ‡ *Fourth Sunday after Pentecost (C)*

Bear One Another's Burdens

GALATIANS 6:1-16

I want to preach this morning on two verses in our Galatians passage that are at obvious odds with one another. First, we read, "Bear one another's burdens," but then just three verses later we hear that "all must carry their own loads." One verse says one thing; the other verse says another thing. One verse is the Law, and the other verse is the Gospel. Both are true. What do I mean by this?

This past week David Brooks wrote an op-ed in the *New York Times* about Bill Wilson, the founder of Alcoholics Anonymous. It's a story about both bearing one's own burden as well as having that burden be borne by another. It is a story about both Law and Gospel:

> On Dec. 14, 1934, a failed stockbroker named Bill Wilson was struggling with alcoholism at a New York City detox center. It was his fourth stay at the center and nothing had worked. This time ... he consulted a friend named Ebby Thacher, who told him to give up drinking and give his life over to the service of God.
>
> Wilson was not a believer, but, later that night, at the

end of his rope, he called out in his hospital room: "If there is a God, let Him show Himself! I am ready to do anything. Anything!"

As Wilson described it, a white light suffused his room and the presence of God appeared. "It seemed to me, in the mind's eye, that I was on a mountain and that a wind not of air but of spirit was blowing," he testified later. "And then it burst upon me that I was a free man."

Wilson never touched alcohol again. He went on to help found Alcoholics Anonymous, which, 75 years later, has some 1.2 million members ...

This is an inspiring story that has both despair and redemption. It is a story of bearing one's own burden, in that Bill Wilson was alone in that hospital room bearing the consequences of his own choices. There was no escape, no one else to blame. That is the Law at work. And yet it is also a story of another bearing Bill's burden for him— God coming to him in white light and setting him free. That is the Gospel at work.

I want to suggest this morning that Bill Wilson's story is in some way everyone's story. Although not everyone is an alcoholic, his story has universal connection. This is because addiction is the best way to describe our sinful condition as human beings. As I said, we are not all addicted to alcohol or drugs or sex, but we are all addicted to self because of our original sin. Our addictions can take many forms: you can be addicted to your success; you can be addicted to control; you can be addicted to your children; you can be addicted to Fourth of July sales; you can be addicted to anger or lust or envy. You can even be addicted to getting positive feedback on your sermons!

Our dog Blue keeps getting into the compost bucket on our porch. As you might imagine the compost bucket smells terrible— terrible to us, but apparently not terrible to Blue. We thought we had secured the lid, but Blue continues to find a way to nose the top off the bucket and dig into coffee grounds, rotting onions, and broken chicken eggs. Of course, his culinary escapades result in his general discomfort and being sick to his stomach at all hours of the night, but that doesn't stop him from the next round. He just can't help it.

The Bible says that when it comes to sin, we are like Blue. Sin is terrible for us, makes us sick, leads to our general discomfort and even to our death, but we return to whatever version of the compost bucket dominates our lives. There is actually a Bible verse that describes this: "Like a dog that returns to its vomit / is a fool who reverts to his folly." You may be thinking, "OK, fine, but I'm no fool." You may be thinking that, but the Bible thinks otherwise. The writer of Ecclesiastes says,

> The wise have eyes in their head,
>   but fools walk in darkness.
> Yet I perceived that the same fate befalls all of them.

God has put into our universe this inexorable Law that cannot be violated. The Law says that we all must bear our own burden. Paul also say it this way in our Galatians reading: "Do not be deceived; God is not mocked, for you reap whatever you sow."

Just as in a garden, if you plant a tomato seed, you will harvest a tomato and not a cucumber. If you sow anger and irritation toward your children, you will reap resentment and distance when they grow up. If you sow licentiousness in your dating life you will reap distrust from your future spouse, and perhaps the recompense of disease in your body. If you sow avarice in your spending life, you will reap crushing debt.

You reap what you sow. This is the Law, and in a real way, you must bear these consequences alone. There is no use in soft-pedaling the brunt of the Law. But then again, I don't need to because you have your own compost bucket to tell you the exact same thing.

If all we had was God's Law, life would be very grim indeed. We would only inhabit the despairing first part of Bill Wilson's story. That is what the Law is intended to do, to drive us to despair in ourselves. Drive us to the end of our rope. Drive us to a hospital room and drop us off in the middle of the night. As Paul says, the law condemns us.

This is an alien word for our culture because we are generally taught to avoid despair and weakness and need. Yet this is how God works. This is also how AA works and what Bill Wilson discovered that night at the end of his rope in 1943. David Brooks rightly notes,

"In a culture that generally celebrates empowerment and self-esteem, AA begins with disempowerment. The goal is to get people to gain control over their lives, but it all begins with an act of surrender and an admission of weakness."

The act of surrender and the admission of weakness are the doorway from the Law to the Gospel, God's word of mercy and love for sinners who repeatedly go back to the compost bucket. Along with the Law, there is the Gospel: "Bear one another's burdens, and in this way you will fulfill the law of Christ." Sometimes you can't make it on your own.

Bearing another's burdens is not simple or clean. At the end of Norman Maclean's *A River Runs Through It*, an old father talks with his son about how to help his other son. The one son has a penchant for alcohol, street fighting and reckless living. The father is a minister, with a lifetime of experience on trying to bear one another's burdens:

> "Help," he said, "is giving a part of yourself to somebody who comes to accept it willingly and needs it badly.
>
> "So it is ... that we can seldom help anybody. Either we don't know what part to give or maybe we don't like to give any part of ourselves. Then, more often than not, the part that is needed is not wanted. And even more often, we do not have the part that is needed. It is like the auto-supply shop over town where they always say, 'Sorry, we are just out of that part.'"
>
> I told him, "You make it too tough. Help doesn't have to be anything that big."

To bear one another's burdens is to admit weakness as the norm for our lives. It is to both give help and receive help. Bearing one another's burdens is infused with the Gospel because it is predicated on recognition of weakness and is actuated by love and mercy. It is also the way to be real with each other. Again, David Brooks says,

> In a culture that thinks of itself as individualistic, AA relies on fellowship. The general idea is that people aren't really captains of their own ship. Successful members become

deeply intertwined with one another—learning, sharing, suffering, and mentoring one another. Individual repair is a social effort.

Scriptures today tells us, "all must carry their own loads." This is the law that is inexorable and true. But it also tells us, "Bear one another's burdens." Often it is true that we don't have the right part or we don't like to give any part of ourselves. Sometimes we can and do help one another. It is in these times that we feel most alive and we feel close to one another.

Ultimately, though, the burden of our addiction to sin is too big to be borne by ourselves or even by others relating to us in love. This burden must be borne by another, by one who has the parts that are needed and who gives of himself. When Bill Wilson cried out, "If there is a God, let Him show Himself," that prayer was answered in Jesus Christ, the Lamb of God who takes away the sin of the world. God knew what part to give: He gave himself to die on the cross for your addictions. Jesus bore his own load of despair and humiliation. No one else could do it. Individual repair was his own effort. And in doing so, he bore your burden and thus fulfilled the law of Christ.

Amen.

July 3, 2011 ‡ *Fifth Sunday after Pentecost (A)*

I Do Not Do What I Want To Do

ROMANS 7:15-25

Today's lectionary reading from Paul's letter to the Romans is among my favorite passages. One reason I love this passage is that I can relate so deeply to it. When I read, "I do not understand my own actions. For I do not do what I want, but I do the very thing I hate. ... I can will what is right, but I cannot do it," I feel completely understood. I feel understood by Paul, by the Bible, and of course, by God, who inspired these words. I feel as though Paul is inside my very skin, inhabiting my own life, struggling just the way I struggle.

I've met very few people who don't instinctively relate to this passage. People struggle with a divided self. Paul says, "I find it to be a law that when I want to do what is good, evil lies close at hand." It's so true to experience. This is why we laugh at John Belushi in *Animal House*, as he sits with an angel on one shoulder and a devil on the other, each whispering in his ears. Paul's description, I believe, is a universal description of human internal conflict. In his words, he is "at war" with himself.

Does this realistic but grim description of the weakness of our will mean that we can never will what is right and actually do it? Of course not. It just means that everyone has areas where his or her will is compromised, where he or she is vulnerable to forces that defy self-control. It just means that there are pockets, sometimes deep pockets, in a person's life where "I do not do what I want, but do the very thing that I hate."

What are your pockets? For many people this hits home in the appetites. You really have no business putting that extra expense on your credit card, but in the moment, you just feel that you cannot live without that purchase. You do not want that extra weight, but you just cannot do what you need to do to lose it. You should not have that third drink, fourth drink, but you just can't seem to put the bottle away. In these situations, the diabolical voice of the divided self sounds so reasonable and funny. (To justify her daytime bourbon, one of my relatives use to say, "Well, it's dark under the porch!")

Well, let's say that you're one of those disciplined and self-controlled people who runs 10 miles at 5 am and then sits down to some granola and green tea for breakfast. The passions may not be your downfall, but you also have pockets in your life that reveal your compromised will. Maybe worry is a pocket that will not bend to your own control. You don't want to worry. You know that worrying accomplishes nothing, that it disrupts your sleep and affects your health. You even know that God himself commands you not to worry—"be anxious for nothing," he says—and still, you worry about all kinds of things, keeping you up at night and upsetting your days. As author Ian McEwan says, "No one can predict which of life's vexations insomnia will favor. Even in daylight, in optimal conditions, one rarely exercises a free choice over what to fret about."

The pockets Jesus chose to point out in the Sermon on the Mount are anger and lust. Jesus goes right to the heart, doesn't he? He goes right to the sin that wells up despite us, and right to the place out of which those sins arise. For many people, anger lurks low and constant, tamped down but never out, always waiting for a chance to spring out like a caged lion. That chance comes when you are cut off while you're driving, or when your sense of personal justice is violated, or when you're exhausted from worry and loosened up by your third drink. What's there all along comes out.

William Inge was a playwright from the 50s to the 70s. In his play *Come Back, Little Sheba*, the main character Doc is a recovering alcoholic married to a woman who was quite beautiful when she was young, but she has "let herself go" and feels slobby and old at age 39. Doc seems to cope with his career and marriage disappointments when he is sober, but then he relapses. When the whiskey talks, he tears into his wife, the torrent of anger and frustration erupting like a volcano. He does the very thing he hates and hurts the very one who loves him.

Lust is almost too obvious a target to expound upon. We'll just let Jesus' words from the Sermon on the Mount speak for themselves: "You have heard that it was said, 'You shall not commit adultery.' But I say to you that everyone who looks at a woman with lust has already committed adultery with her in his heart." As Bono sings, "But every time she passes by / Wild thoughts escape."

"For I do not do what I want, but I do the very thing that I hate." I haven't even touched on depression or real addiction, but I hope you see that you are in the same boat as I am, the boat of humanity shot through with leaks. On the waters of life, we are not an entirely seaworthy species.

It is crucial that we honestly see our own vulnerabilities, because this leads us to the second reason this passage is so affecting. It is the very center of a theology of compassion for other people. If you believe that another person should be able to "straighten up and fly right" if they apply enough will power or discipline or gumption to whatever it is that is vexing them, then you will inevitably be frustrated with that person's continuing shabby behavior.

Here's a little test to gauge your compassion for others, or lack thereof. Any time you catch yourself thinking or saying, "I just can't believe a person could do that," or "I don't understand how he could treat her that way," or "OK, that's going too far. How on earth could he have done that? I just don't get it," then you have failed to understand human nature. And you have not just failed to understand human nature in a general way, but you have failed to understand human nature in a very specific way—your own human nature! You have conveniently overlooked your own problems. Jesus has something to say about this, too. "You hypocrite, first take the log out of your own eye, and then you will see clearly to take the speck out of your neighbor's eye." Ripe sarcasm there from Jesus.

If you see the other person through the lens of scripture, then you will see, through the log of your own eye, a person just like yourself: someone who isn't freely choosing to fly off the handle or drink too much or talk incessantly or struggle with anxiety. You will see someone who is acted upon by forces deep and dark, someone, like you, whose will is compromised. I've never met anyone who wakes up and says, "OK, today I will choose to be depressed! Today I will choose to be angry! Today, I will choose to alienate everyone around me!"

Compassion is what people need. It is what I need, and it is what you need. I have a friend from my Alabama days who is in federal prison. She committed a terrible crime. No question about it. It is the kind of crime that you can't even mention in prison. She wrote me that she has to keep what she did to herself or lie about it because if she came clean she would be ostracized or even harmed by the other prisoners.

My friend in prison needs compassion, and you need compassion in the pockets of your own prisons. We need compassion on the receiving end, but also on the giving end. And if we have any hope to be compassionate to others, it will come from recognizing our own compromised will. We're in this together. "Blessed are the merciful, for they shall receive mercy."

Today is the 27th anniversary of the day I wrecked my car as a 19-year-old, causing my best friend to lose his right eye. That day was an extreme case of my doing the very thing I hate. I was driving recklessly, but of course I did not want to hurt the very one I loved. And you probably know how the story ended. I walked into Drew's hospital room a few days after the wreck, and he said, "Paul, I love you and forgive you. I could have been driving." In fact, Drew was always a safe driver, but he said what he said for my sake. "Blessed are the merciful, for they will receive mercy."

The final reason this passage is so powerful is Paul's conclusion, the only safe harbor to which the boat of humanity is bound: "Wretched man that I am! Who will rescue me from this body of death?"

You know the answer. You know the only hope for hurting people. You know the One who has compassion on sinners. You know the One who shows you mercy. You know the One who willed what was right and did what was right for your sake. You know the One who is waiting there for you, on the backside of your anger or lust or worry or judgment. "Who will rescue me from this body of death? Thanks be to God through Jesus Christ our Lord!"

Amen.

July 14, 2019 ‡ *Fifth Sunday after Pentecost (C)*

Hell in the Parking Lot

COLOSSIANS 1:1-14

B efore the Apostle Paul was the Apostle Paul, he was Saul, a man who fiercely persecuted Christians. But one day when he was on horseback on the road to Damascus, the risen Christ appeared to him, saying "Saul, Saul, why do you persecute me?" Saul was literally knocked off his high horse and blinded by the light.

While Saul was lying on the ground, unable to see, Jesus gave Saul his new mission in life. He said,

> But get up and stand on your feet; for I have appeared to you for this purpose, to appoint you to serve and testify to the things in which you have seen me and to those in which I will appear to you ... to open [people's] eyes so that they may turn from darkness to light and from the power of Satan to God, so that they may receive forgiveness of sins and a place among those who are sanctified by faith in me.

Saul became the Apostle Paul, the chief articulator of the glorious Gospel of Jesus Christ.

We hear a direct reference to his Damascus Road experience

in this morning's reading from Colossians. Paul tells his group of fledgling Christians that God "has rescued us from the power of darkness and transferred us into the kingdom of his beloved Son, in whom we have redemption, the forgiveness of sins." That is a clear reprisal of Jesus' charge to him while he was lying on the ground in darkness.

There are certain passages of Scripture that efficiently articulate the Gospel, and today's passage is one of them. Remember, the Gospel is not an adjective—'Gospel music' or 'Gospel truth.' The Gospel is not a call to action—"the Gospel compels you to do so-and-so." The Gospel is not a genre of literature—"a reading from the Gospel of Mark."

Instead, the Gospel is news. It is an announcement of something that has already happened—"the US women's soccer team won the World Cup for the fourth time." Now, you may like the US women's soccer team, you may dislike the US Women's soccer team, you may not care about the US women's soccer team, you may have never heard of the US women's soccer team, or of the sport called soccer, or of the country called the United States. None of that matters. None of that has any bearing on the fact, the news, that last Sunday, July 7, 2019, the US women's soccer team won the World Cup.

Like that announcement, the Gospel is news. Specifically, the Gospel is *good* news. And more specifically, the Gospel is good news about God and people. In Paul's iteration of that good news in his letter to the Colossians, it is the announcement that God has "rescued us." Specifically, "He has rescued us from the power of darkness."

Let's pause there to peer into the power of darkness. But let's not pause too long or peer too keenly because the power of darkness will make us shudder. Remember that the Bible's worldview recognizes the presence of an active malevolence. This is why the first question a baptismal candidate is asked is, "Do you renounce Satan and all the spiritual forces of wickedness that rebel against God?" It's followed by, "Do you renounce all the evil powers of this world which corrupt and destroy the creatures of God?"

What is the power of darkness? With the new season of Stranger Things, and the plethora of superhero movies, there are plenty of cinematic depictions of the more obvious powers of darkness, which seek to corrupt and destroy the creatures of God. These "powers and principalities," as the Bible calls them, are real. But let me give you a more relatable illustration of the power of darkness's endgame. Robert Capon, our favorite theologian, describes his vision of hell. It is a description that has convicting power for those of us here on earth:

> the neat spirit of hell is a championing of the right so profound that it produces a permanent unwillingness to forgive, an eternal conviction that wrong should be prevented whenever possible and punished whenever not, but that it must never under any circumstances be absolved ... That is the hell of hell. That's why it's presided over by the rightest angel who ever lived.

If you are a person who always has to be right, or a person who has to see justice done, you know the neat satisfaction of seeing wrongdoers punished or having the truth vindicated. The world needs this to happen to stay on its axis. But you also know the personal toll that having to be right exacts on a relationship.

I found this out in the Christ Church parking lot. If you've ever attempted to park at Christ Church, not just on a Sunday, but at any hour of any day, you know it is next to impossible. I have to admit that sometimes during the week I take a perverse pleasure in catching transgressors trying to park in our lot. I'm happy for parishioners to use it, but it drives me nuts when random people ignore our signs and take up one of our 18 spaces. It's just not right.

At the end of a particularly tiring day, I caught a young couple leaving their car and walking to the downtown mall. I have to say, I kind of lit into them: "MAY I HELP YOU? ARE YOU HERE ON CHURCH BUSINESS? CAN'T YOU READ THE SIGNS?" I only stopped my harangue because it dawned on me who they were—a young couple I really liked and who had started coming to Christ Church on Sundays at my invitation to hear the preacher preach about the grace of God. I had been very excited that they were in church. Despite my apology to them in the parking lot, you already will have guessed that the previous Sunday was their *last* Sunday ever at Christ Church.

On that note, we'll move on to the second part of Paul's Gospel announcement. Having rescued us from the power of darkness, God has "transferred us into the kingdom of his beloved Son, in whom we have redemption, the forgiveness of sins." Again, Capon gives us a glimpse of this kingdom into which we have been transferred:

> though earth can sometimes indeed be heaven, it can never quite manage to be pure hell: there is always the chance that out of pure feeblemindedness if nothing else we might just drop the subject of being right.
>
> ... Heaven is not the home of the good but of the forgiven forgivers; ... everybody in heaven, God himself included, has decided to die to the question of who's wrong; whereas nobody in hell can even shut up about who's right.

As an illustration of this new kingdom, there is moving scene in the novel *The Overstory*, which won the 2019 Pulitzer Prize for fiction. A woman comes to see a therapist who has a thriving practice but a highly unusual method: she and her client look directly at one another, locking eyes and not saying a word for three full hours. Strange, right? Try staring at another person for more than six seconds. Most people, even newly in love people, find it too intimidating and intimate to hold the gaze.

But the therapy works. Her waiting list is a mile long. The session described in the novel includes the thoughts going through the patient Stephanie's head, thoughts like, "Do I make sense to you? Am I much like everyone else?" The tensions builds:

> At half an hour, Stephanie melts down. She's hungry, stiff, itchy, and so sick of herself she wants to sleep forever. The truth seeps out of her, a bodily discharge. *You shouldn't trust me. I don't deserve this. You see? I'm [messed] up in ways even my children don't suspect.*

What the therapist does, and why her therapy works, is to look directly at her clients without judgment for as long as they need. Finally, after three hours, Stephanie (and the therapist) burst into tears: "Who are you? Why won't you stop? No one has ever looked at me like this, except to judge ... In my whole life, my whole life, never."

The kingdom of God's beloved Son is not the realm of the good but of the forgiven. And that's because on the cross of Christ, the Lord decided to die to the question of who's wrong. In fact, it is we, all of us who were wrong, who were blinded by the power of darkness. But in his mercy, God has rescued us in Christ Jesus, in whom we have the forgiveness of sins.

I'll close with a prayer from the Daily Devotions for noon, in our Book of Common Prayer. This one could sum up the Apostle Paul's mission to the world. As we're seated, let us pray: "Blessed Savior, at this hour you hung upon the cross, stretching out your loving arms: Grant that all the peoples of the earth may look to you and be saved; for your tender mercies' sake. Amen."

July 21, 2013 ‡ *Sixth Sunday after Pentecost (C)*

What You Need Is What Will Last

LUKE 10:38-42

The Rolling Stones sang, "You can't always get what you want, / But if you try sometimes you just might find / You get what you need." In this morning's Gospel, Mary finds that she gets what she needs. As some translations say, she gets the "one thing needful." She gets something that can never be taken away from her.

Jesus and his friends are at Martha and Mary's house for dinner. Martha is rushing around getting the hors d'oeuvres together, laying out the china, marinating the lamb chops. As usual, she had already been the one to plan the menu, do the grocery shopping, vacuum the house, and iron the napkins. She was the one who made sure the guest bedroom was in order and the sink in the hall bathroom had been cleaned. It was bad enough that their brother Lazarus had spent the day on the golf course and would waltz in just in time for cocktails, but that's what she expected of a man.

But Mary was another story. Her sister really steamed her. While she had been working her fingers to the bone, what had her younger sister been doing? Absolutely nothing, just sitting around talking with Jesus and his friends, as if dinner for 16 would just magically appear on the table! All the tension of the day and the irritation at her sister continues to build. Martha hears yet another gale of laughter coming from the living room while she is alone in the kitchen buttering the peas. Finally, she snaps. Martha rushes into the living room, apron over her dress, one hand on her hip, the other pointing not at Mary, but at Jesus.

She's furious with her sister, but she decides to triangulate, venting to Jesus. Of all people, the Teacher should care about duty and responsibility! After all, Martha polished the silver and cut fresh flowers for him. She makes a scene, interrupting the story Jesus is telling, and demands, "Lord, do you not care that my sister has left me to do all the work by myself?" Then she instructs Jesus to adjudicate the family dispute: "Tell her then to help me." She's so angry she can't even say Mary's name!

Awkward silence. The disciples are embarrassed and look down at their feet. Mary sits stock-still. The only sound is the potatoes that are starting to boil over in the kitchen. How would Jesus answer? Well, like all wise people, Jesus refuses to be triangulated, especially in between two sisters. His answer is directly to Martha. "Martha, Martha, you are worried and distracted by many things; there is need of only one thing. Mary has chosen the better part, which will not be taken away from her." I'll leave it for you to imagine how Martha responds to *that* answer!

This story generally peeves and vexes a certain kind of person. People who take umbrage with this story are also bothered by Jesus' parable about the vineyard workers: some worked for 15 minutes in the cool of the evening and got paid the same as those who worked 10 hours in the blaze of the sun. Maybe that was the very story Jesus was telling Mary and his disciples when Martha stormed in. Yet in this scene, Mary doesn't get the same pay as Martha. Mary, who does nothing, gets the *better* part; she gets what is needed and lasting in life. Martha, who does everything, gets nothing but high blood pressure.

The affront to industrious, responsible activity here is too obvious to elaborate on. Again, did Mary think that dinner for 16 would just magically appear on the table? Well, who knows, really? Maybe she did, and maybe it would! After all, the guest of honor did feed 5,000 hungry people with five loaves of bread and two fish. What could he have done with Martha's smoked salmon and sesame crackers?

Jesus calls Martha's work a distraction that causes her worry. She's so distracted that she's missing out on what is important and permanent in life, or as Jesus says, "one thing is needful ... which shall not be taken away." What are our distractions? Any and everything can be used as a distraction from what is needed and lasting in life. As Jesus says, Martha is distracted by "many things." In Martha's case, even serving the Lord is a distraction, quite literally.

What are our distractions? I can't help but mention the Internet in general and smart phones in particular. I have one, and it is extremely useful and helpful. But what a distraction! How many times do parents of teenagers have to say "put your phone away!" only to then pull out their own phones when they buzz with a text? Texting and all its variations is how ninth graders communicate with each other while in the backseat of the same car. It's absurd that Virginia had to pass a law against texting while driving. How could anyone think they could text and drive at the same time? It shows how deeply engrained this current distraction is in us.

But phones are not the problem, obviously. We are. Pascal famously wrote in his *Pensées*, "I have discovered that all the unhappiness of men arises from one single fact, that they cannot stay quietly in their own chamber." And that was in the 1600s. The human heart hasn't changed from Martha's time to Pascal's time to ours. The human heart craves what it has always craved: security and affirmation. People check their emails and text messages and Facebook pages all the time because each message or text delivers the possibility of affirmation. A recent study showed that receiving emails and texts work on our brain in the same way as drug or alcohol or sex addiction.

The problem is that the affirmation never lasts, and phones can be taken away and hidden in drawers. What Jesus calls a distraction is just that—it distracts us for a moment. But then the dinner party is over and all you're left with is dirty dishes. Or your work finally becomes boring and ceases to be a strong enough distraction. Or your spouse finally can't bear the burden of being responsible for your affirmation and security. In and through all your nonstop activity, you still wake up in the morning and feel empty inside.

Jesus tells Martha that there is a different way, a better way to live. Mary's way, to do nothing, to sit down in front of Jesus and listen to what he is saying, is what a person needs in life and what lasts in life. Jesus could have been quoting the psalmist: "Be still, and know that I am God." Notice, it's not "Be busy and act like you are God." Maybe he told the old joke: What is the difference between you and God? God never pretends that he is you!

Mary doing absolutely nothing but sitting and receiving is the perfect example of what Martin Luther called "passive righteousness." As he wrote, "For in the righteousness of faith, we work nothing, render nothing unto God, but we only receive, and suffer another to work in us, that is to say, God." As for the passing and ephemeral distraction of our own activity, Luther wisely wrote, "I could not trust in it ... [therefore I] embrace only that passive righteousness which is the righteousness of grace, mercy, and forgiveness of sins."

The love of God is what your heart craves. The love of God is what gives you security and affirmation. The love of God is the one needful thing. And the love of God can never be taken away from you, for love never ends and love never fails. And what do you have to do to get this love of God? You have to do nothing. As Mary and Martha show us this morning, you have to do nothing. All the somethings in your life will one day be taken away from you. Everything will disappear except the one thing needful—God's love for you in Jesus Christ, his grace, mercy, and forgiveness of sins.

I said that Mary is the perfect example. The problem is that most of us aren't perfect examples. If I stopped there, then I would have just given you good advice that you won't follow anyway. That's not the Gospel. The Gospel is that most of us are Marthas who have trouble being still and knowing that he is God. I'll close with an illustration of how God comes after all of us who are worried and distracted, those of us who do not choose the better part.

My minister friend Jim shares the story of a boy named Earl, whom he met at summer camp. Earl's only method of coping with the difficulties in his life was anger. He acted out, he fought with campers, he threw food in the dining hall. Jim recalls,

> One evening, the entire camp was gathered together for a
> campfire. We were singing a song when, out of the corner of

my eye, I saw Earl sneaking up behind a camper that he especially hated. Before I could do anything, Earl kicked the boy in the back, hard. Then he took off, running through the woods.

The camp director that summer was a man named "Bibs," and he was a wonderful man who knew about angry distractions and who also knew about the cross. Bibs saw the entire scene at the campfire. Like a shot, he charged after Earl. I followed them and saw Bibs catch up with Earl. Bibs put his arms around Earl from behind, pinned his arms to his sides, lifted him off the ground and just held him.

I have never seen such kicking and screaming and swearing. It seemed to go on for hours. Bibs didn't say a word. He just kept hugging Earl. Slowly, the kicking and swearing died down. Then there was silence. Then, somehow, Earl managed to squirm around in Bibs' arms. He threw his arms around Bibs' neck and sobbed and sobbed and sobbed. Bibs just held him and hugged him.

The love of God is the one thing needful and the one thing that can never be taken away. What you need is what will last.

Amen.

August 13, 2017 ‡ *Tenth Sunday after Pentecost (A)*

Jesus Comes Aboard the Ship of Fools

MATTHEW 14:22-33

Two nights prior, hundreds of white nationalists rallied at the University of Virginia carrying torches. The next day, they arrived downtown at a statue of Robert E. Lee to protest plans to remove it. Violence erupted, and later that afternoon a car drove into a crowd of counter-protestors, killing one person and wounding many others. The statue, which remains in place, is directly adjacent to Christ Church.

I'm grateful to see you all here this morning. I know that some have stayed away from downtown, fearing lingering violence. Yesterday was a terrible day for Charlottesville. I hope that here you can receive a message of hope and comfort.

You probably assume that you are sitting in the sanctuary of Christ Church, but in fact, you are not. You are actually sitting in the *nave* of Christ Church. The nave is the central part of the church starting at the narthex, where you entered the church, and extending to the altar rail. Inside the altar rail are the chancel and the sanctuary.

Why is the main part of the church called the nave? It takes its name for the Latin word *navis*, meaning ship, vessel, or boat. That is the source of the word "navy" in English. You may not have realized that you've come aboard when you walked through those red doors to sit down in your pew. But tilt your head and look up. Have you ever noticed that our vaulted roof is designed to look like an inverted keel?

The reason for this is not that the gothic church architects were yachtsman but that early on the Church identified itself as a boat. As early as the second century, the Church saw itself as a ship tossed on the sea of disbelief, worldliness, and persecution. The Church is a vessel meant to reach safe harbor with its cargo of human souls. A boat was also a useful symbol during times when the persecuted Church needed to disguise the cross, since the ship's mast is shaped like one.

There are two scripture references for the Church as ship. The first is Noah's ark. Frederick Buechner says the resemblance is worth thinking about:

> In one as in the other, just about everything imaginable is aboard, the clean and the unclean both. They are all piled in together helter-skelter, the predators and the prey, the wild and the tame, the sleek and beautiful ones and the ones that are ugly as sin. There are sly young foxes and impossible old cows. There are the catty and the piggish and the peacock-proud. There are hawks and there are doves. Some are wise as owls, some silly as geese; some meek as lambs and others ravening wolves. There are times when they all cackle and grunt and roar and sing together, and there are times when you could hear a pin drop. Most of them have no clear idea just where they're supposed to be heading or how they're supposed to get there or what they'll find if and when they finally do ...
>
> It's not all enjoyable. There's backbiting just like everywhere else. There's a pecking order. There's jostling at the trough. There's growling and grousing, bitching and whining. There are dogs in the manger and old goats and black widows. It's a regular menagerie in there, and sometimes it smells to high heaven like one.
>
> But even at its worst, there's at least one thing that

> makes it bearable within, and that is the storm without—the wild winds and terrible waves and in all the watery waste, no help in sight.
>
> And if there is never clear sailing, there is at least shelter from the blast, a sense of somehow heading in the right direction in spite of everything, a ship to keep afloat, and, like a beacon in the dark, the hope of finding safe harbor at last.

The one thing that makes it bearable within is the storm without. We've had quite the storm blowing without, all directly around Christ Church. As I said, yesterday was a terrible day for Charlottesville. And it has enraged and frightened and unsettled people from all across the spectrum—the doves and the hawks, the wolves and the lambs alike. After the torch-lit march on the Lawn Friday night, the ever-measured, deeply respected Larry Sabato said that he had never seen anything of its kind in his 47-year association with the University. The Lawn, he said, was in need of an exorcism.

In my opinion, the storm without makes it not just *bearable* within the inverted keel of Christ Church, but *lifesaving*. With the storm without raging from all sides, never is it more crucial for the nave of Christ Church to be a kind of sanctuary, a safe place. As Dylan sings, "Try imagining a place where it's always safe and warm / 'Come in,' she said, 'I'll give you shelter from the storm.'"

The storm is blowing without in the our second Scripture reference for the church as a ship. In today's Gospel, we read that the disciples are in a "boat, battered by the waves," now "far from the land, for the wind was against them." Storms are nothing new, of course. And we all have a private catalogue of storms making us feel battered, far from the land, with the wind against us. To be in this world is to be subject to storms. During seminary, a retired navy commander used to say to me and my friend Drew, "I wish you fair winds and smooth sailing." I'm a big fan of fair winds and smooth sailing. Unfortunately, life does not always cooperate.

Like the disciples in story, I am desperately in need of Jesus to come to me walking on the water. We all need Jesus to get into the boat to take the helm. If Jesus Christ isn't at the helm, then we are all sailing on a ship of fools.

Before Jesus gets in the boat and takes the helm, the disciples see him and think he is a ghost. Jesus assures them, saying "Take heart; it is I. Do not be afraid." Peter, with his usual bravado, says, "Lord, if it is you, command me to come to you on the water." He gets out of the boat, takes a few steps, then down he goes.

He then cries out something that is true and real and universal. He cries out the very thing you and I cry out in the face of the battering waves and prevailing wind. He cries out the one thing I want you to remember from this sermon, the one true recognition of our human predicament. And it is the true recognition of God's mighty power. Peter, sinking down, sinking down, cries out, "Lord, save me!"

Lord, save me! is a prayer to pray night and day. *Lord, save me!* is the right response to the storms of life. And *Lord, save us!* feels like the right prayer to pray in Charlottesville, Virginia, this Sunday morning.

Jesus does save Peter. Then he comes aboard the ship of fools. Then the winds cease, the waves recede, and the storm dies down. They then sail, presumably, to the other side of the sea in peace and calm. But since in life we are subject to storms, the peace and the calm do not last. It certainly doesn't last for Jesus.

Jesus only temporarily answers *Lord, save me!* by lifting Peter up from the drowning waves and taking him aboard the wooden ship. He fully and finally satisfies that plea not in the wooden boat but on the wooden cross. Jesus saves Peter, Jesus saves you and me, Jesus saves the world, by not saving himself.

Week in and week out, storms within and storms without, it is always lifesaving to come into this nave, settle into your berth, and hear once again the never-changing word of the Gospel for all people: Jesus Christ died for the sin of the whole world. On the wooden cross, death and evil and hatred are defeated. He rose from the grave to take us to safe harbor at last.

Lord, save me! we say. "Come in," he says, "I'll give you shelter from the storm."

Amen.

August 25, 2013 ‡ *Eleventh Sunday after Pentecost (C)*

A-Rod, Ahab, and the Daughter of Abraham

LUKE 13:10-17

My son and I are Red Sox fans. We watched the Red Sox play the Yankees last Sunday night. I think nearly everyone knows that the Yankees and the Red Sox are arch-rivals. Of course, we were rooting with all our might for the Sox, but something happened at Fenway Park that curbed our enthusiasm.

Alex Rodriguez, who plays for the Yankees, stepped up to bat. A-Rod, as he's known, is a baseball megastar, with 649 home runs, only a little more than 100 behind the major league record. A-Rod, however, has been accused of using performance-enhancing drugs, a charge which neither he nor his lawyers have yet to deny, and a charge which results in suspension from the league. According to Major League Baseball rules, an accused player may continue playing while he is appealing the charge. This is what A-Rod is doing, and therefore they allowed him to step to the plate.

Of course, he was booed vociferously. But then it went a step farther. Ryan Dempster, the pitcher, intentionally threw at A-Rod on the first pitch. The ball actually went behind him. OK, message sent. But then the second and third pitches were up and inside, causing Alex to veer out of the way. Then the fourth pitch was a fastball aimed right at the batter that hit him squarely on the elbow. The crowd cheered like the Sox had won the World Series. No matter what you think about A-Rod, that incident is unsettling. I was glad when Rodriguez hit a home run later in the game—a little instant karma.

Maybe if I'd been there, I would have been caught up in the moment and cheered the pitcher, too. Mob mentality does take over. But what's behind that mob mentality? I wonder if A-Rod was just a scapegoat for all the frustrations, petty and otherwise, felt by the Boston crowd that night. Domestic arguments, professional slights, traffic cut-offs, basic unhappiness—did all these find expression in Dempster's intentionally violent pitch?

I think we see this dynamic in our Gospel passage today. Jesus is teaching in the synagogue on the Sabbath day. A poor crippled woman walks in. She's been hunched over for 18 years, presumably in constant physical pain. Jesus sees her, stops what he's doing or saying, calls her over and heals her. This compassionate work of God creates the usual antagonism among the authorities. As the text says, they were "indignant because Jesus had cured on the sabbath." No surprise: we're pretty well versed in the use of religion against people, of ideology and institution over the needs of the individual.

What caught my attention this time around in this passage was the authorities' response: "There are six days on which work ought to be done; come on those days and be cured, and not on the sabbath day." This abstemious comment seems to be directed at the poor, suffering woman.

Really? This daughter of Abraham is healed after 18 years of pain and the religionists are nitpicking about on which day of the week it happens? She's been curved in on herself, unable to look another person in the eye for 6,570 days, and she chose the wrong day for healing? And she didn't even choose it! She didn't ask to be healed. Jesus, the friend of sinners, the one "whose property is always to have mercy," sees her suffering and responds.

I think there is serious transference happening here with this bent over woman. We tend to scapegoat the strange. Racism and homophobia are obvious examples. And don't we tend to hate in others the very thing we hate in ourselves? When we bristle at the ego in someone else, vilifying them as narcissistic, I wonder if we are transferring our own narcissism onto the other, trying to deal with what is ugly in ourselves.

Parents are usually hardest on the children who exhibit the bad qualities that they find in themselves. Our daughter has her learner's permit and is driving. I tend to do a lot of yelling when I'm in the car with her. What do I yell about? Of course, the very things I do wrong when I drive!

This scapegoating dynamic is at the heart of Moby Dick, considered one of the greatest American novels. Melville describes Captain Ahab's consuming obsession with Moby Dick:

> The White Whale swam before him as the monomaniac incarnation of all those malicious agencies which some deep men feel eating in them, till they are left living on with half a heart and half a lung. That intangible malignity which has been from the beginning ...

Ahab locates in the White Whale not just his own malignity, but the sum total of the world's woes:

> All that most maddens and torments; all that stirs up the lees of things; all truth with malice in it; all that cracks the sinews and cakes the brain; all the subtle demonisms of life and thought; all evil, to crazy Ahab, were visibly personified, and made practically assailable in Moby Dick. He piled upon the whale's white hump the sum of all the general rage and hate felt by his whole race from Adam down ...

Moby Dick is Ahab's 'scape-whale.'

The curved in woman in the synagogue is booed like A-Rod and has piled upon her already bent frame the rage and hate felt by the whole race from Adam down. What is deeply telling is the woman's particular malady. Her body, in a dark twist on the definition of a sacrament, is an outward and visible sign of our inward and spiritual condition. Martin Luther described our inner life as "*incurvatus in se*," Latin for "turned in on oneself." Basically, we tend to live inward, toward and for ourselves, rather than outward, toward and for others and God. And a life lived this way never leads to fulfillment and often leads to bitterness. When the authorities see the bent-over woman, they see an expression of themselves.

It's doubtful they recognize this irony because who really fully recognizes his or her own sin? But who doesn't suffer from *incurvatus in se*? Who isn't bent over like this woman, experiencing the pain of self-orientation? And who doesn't offload his own malignities onto a scapegoat? Who really lives for God and for others, with her lips and with her life? As the hymn we sing says, "If thou iniquities dost mark, / Our secret sins and misdeeds dark, / O who shall stand before Thee?"

Although our defenses are high, the Law convicts us all and we are, as the Scripture says "without excuse." This means that people know that there is something wrong, something that needs to be fixed or healed, but it is better and easier to locate that *something wrong* in someone else and not in ourselves.

Maybe deep down we know that we cannot fix ourselves. We need a scapegoat, an A-Rod, a Moby Dick, a poor bent-over daughter of Abraham to take away the malignities eating at us, so that we do not have to go on living with half a lung and half a heart.

The synagogue authorities knew about scapegoating. Every year, on the Day of Atonement, the High Priest would present two goats. One goat, called the Lord's Goat, would be killed and sacrificed to God. This goat represented the burden of the people's collective sin. Its blood was taken behind the veil of the Temple and sprinkled on the Mercy Seat.

Later, the High Priest confessed the sins of the Israelites and placed them figuratively on the head of the other goat, called the scapegoat. This goat was sent into the wilderness, taking the sins away, never to be seen again. The nation's sin was atoned for by the Lord's goat and the scapegoat.

It is impossible to know whether all this was in Jesus' mind as he healed the bent over woman on the Sabbath in the synagogue. By healing the woman, he swayed the crowd who were "rejoicing at all the wonderful things that he was doing." (Mob mentality, thankfully, can swing to the positive side of the ledger.) Yet Jesus knew the prophecy from Isaiah:

All we like sheep have gone astray;

> we have all turned to our own way,
>   and the LORD has laid on him
>   the iniquity of us all.

Jesus is our scapegoat. We cannot fix ourselves, and blaming or scapegoating others only makes things worse. The only one who could stand sinless before God is the one who, for our sake, was "like a lamb that is led to the slaughter." He was sent out of the city gates with our sins. On the cross his blood atones for all that is wrong with you, with me, and the whole race from Adam down.

Amen.

August 16, 2015 ‡ *Twelfth Sunday after Pentecost (B)*

My Wits Begin To Turn

1 KINGS 2:10-12; 3:3-14

In the days before voicemail or smart phones, people had answering machines connected to their landlines. One person's greeting said, "Hello. This is not an answering machine. This is a questioning machine. Your two questions are 1) *Who are you?* and 2) *What do you want?* If you think those questions are easy to answer, you should know that many people spend their entire lives trying to figure out the answers."

Who are you and what do you want? Those questions of identity and desire run deeper than first blush answers like "Paul" and "to fly-fish the River Test in England," or "a minister" and "for lots of people to come to Christ Church on Sundays." *Who are you* and *what do you want* are the questions that undergird our Old Testament passage from 1 Kings today.

King David has died, and King Solomon now reigns on his father's throne. The text says that "Solomon loved the LORD, walking in the statutes of his father David." One night the Lord appears to Solomon in a dream and says, "Ask what I should give you." The story has overtones of the genie in a magic lamp who pops out and tells the finder, "Ask whatever you wish, and I will grant it."

There are plenty of genie-in-a-lamp jokes floating around;

most of them are dirty, but I'll give you a mostly clean one:

> A poor little lonely old lady lived in a house with her cat
> as her only friend. One day the lights went out, since she
> couldn't pay the electric bill, so she went up to the attic and
> got an old oil lamp from her childhood. As she rubbed it
> clean, a genie appeared and allowed her three wishes.
>
> "First," she said, "I want to be so rich I never have to
> worry about money again. Second, I want to be young and
> beautiful. And last, I want you to change my little cat into a
> handsome prince."
>
> As you would expect, there was a loud explosion, with lots
> of thick smoke. As the smoke cleared, she saw that she was
> surrounded by big bags of coins, and that a beautiful young
> woman looked back at her in the mirror. Then she turned as
> her handsome prince walked in the door, held her in his arms,
> and said, "Now I'll bet you're sorry you had me fixed."

Almost all the genie jokes have some kind of moral to the story
punch line, with the asker getting punished for a selfish request. If
the *who are you* turns out to be "a selfish person," and the *what do
you* want is something along the lines of "fame, wealth, and sex ap-
peal," then bad things will happen. In another scenario, a woman
asks a genie to travel around the world with her husband. Hearing
this, the husband asks the genie for a younger traveling compan-
ion. In an instant, *poof!* he ages 20 years.

Solomon has the chance to ask for whatever he wishes. Turns
out that he doesn't ask for health, wealth, or fame for himself. Instead he asks for wisdom, so he can govern God's people with gracious equanimity. This story also has a kind of moral punch line.
God rewards Solomon's selfless request. "Because you have asked
this, and have not asked for yourself long life or riches, or for the
life of your enemies, but have asked for yourself understanding to
discern what is right, I now do according to your word." But, wait!
That's not all! God gives him "riches and honor" as well. He gets a
little prosperity Gospel thrown in for good measure.

In biblical and extra-biblical records, Solomon was rich, famous, and wise. In the most famous account of his wisdom, two

women came before him to resolve a quarrel over which was the true mother of a baby. When Solomon suggested they should divide the living child in two with a sword, one woman said she would rather give the child up than see it killed. Solomon then declared the woman who showed compassion to be the true mother and gave her the baby.

His wealth and fame were such that the Queen of Sheba paid him a royal visit just to see his riches. The Bible says that "King Solomon gave to the queen of Sheba every desire that she expressed." The possible double entendre suggests Solomon's eventual downfall. He had a weakness for women. He had 700 wives and 300 concubines, which does not seem very wise to me. Or to the Lord, as it turns out. To please his foreign wives, Solomon started worshiping their foreign gods, which is a big no-no for the King of Israel. The Lord punishes Solomon by dividing the kingdom posthumously.

The famed wisdom of Solomon begins well but ends badly. He begins focusing outward on others but ends focusing inward on himself. His life is the inverse of another king, King Lear. I read the play yet again when we were in England and its power and profundity—it's wisdom, you might even say—continue to amaze me.

The play opens with Lear in full narcissist mode, dividing his kingdom between his three daughters, demanding full-throated declarations of love from them. The fuller the flattery, the greater the reward. Or so he says, even though he has already made up his mind about who will get what. The two older sisters play the game, while the sainted Cordelia refuses to flatter her father, even though she is the only one who really loves him. Lear is enraged and cuts Cordelia out of the will, sowing the seeds of eventual tragedy.

Once the older sisters get what they want, they ridicule and finally banish their elderly father from their homes. Lear, losing his sanity in his grief, spends a night outside in the lashing rain and the bitter wind. He wants his outward body to feel the pain of his tortured heart. During the awful night, Lear experiences a kind of conversion from obsession with self to care for others. His fool is out in the cold with him, and for the first time, Lear sees him as a person in need:

> My wits begin to turn.
> Come on, my boy: how dost, my boy? art cold?

> I am cold myself. ...
> Poor fool and knave, I have one part in my heart
> That's sorry yet for thee.

Later Lear laments that he didn't care enough about the poor people while he was king. *Who is the king?* At this moment he is a person who cares for others. *What does he want?* He wants shelter from the storm for his fool. Lear dies in the end—it is a tragedy, after all. But he dies reconciled with Cordelia. Unlike Solomon, Lear goes from self to other.

"My wits begin to turn" is a classic expression of repentance. *Metanoia*, the Greek for "repentance," means to turn. As far as I can tell, this is true wisdom. True wisdom is the recognition that chasing after the genie list of selfish goals will end in moral bankruptcy at best and tragedy at worst. Since we are all hardwired for self-glorification, a turning of the wits, a conversion, is necessary. It is usually brought on by heartbreak or hardship, as with King Lear.

When your wits begin to turn, by whatever means, you have a shot at answering the questioning machine. *Who are you?* I am a sinner focused on myself. *What do you want?* I want mercy, forgiveness, and amendment of life.

It is ironic, isn't it, that Lear's turning wit is inspired by the fool, who suffers along side of him in the wet and the cold? That is hardly a new idea. St. Paul tells us that God's foolishness is wiser than the wisdom of the world.

God sent his Son into the world as one who was foolish in the eyes of the world. He had no money to speak of, no advanced degrees, and no political power. Like Lear's fool, he was a suffering servant. The prophet Isaiah says, "he had no form or majesty that we should look at him, / nothing in his appearance that we should desire him." He never married, had no children, and died young.

He talked about losing your life to save it, and giving your stuff away to anyone who asks. He said foolish things like, if someone punches you on one side of your face, turn your other cheek for the next blow. While the world said, "Fool me once, shame on you; fool me twice, shame on me—time to wise up," he said, "If someone hurts, offends, or ridicules you, forgive them each time, over and over and over again."

The wise of the world had had enough of his foolishness and decided to crucify him. The night before he was killed, Jesus asked God to take this cup of suffering away from him. But his wish was not granted. The wise scorned him, calling him the king of the Jews and mocking him with a crown of thorns. He was exposed to the elements, stripped and flouted, turned out from his own people, who said, "We have no king but Caesar." Unlike the child whom Solomon's wisdom saved, God's child was killed. When he died, he was buried in a borrowed tomb.

But the foolishness of God is wiser than the wisdom of the world, and on the third day Jesus was raised from the dead. Not only does his foolish wisdom live on 2,000 years after his death, but he lives on. In fact, he speaks still today, saying, "Behold, I stand at the door, and knock." Were you to open that door and ask, "Who are you and what do you want?" he would answer, "I am your Savior, and I want you."

Amen.

August 28, 2016 ‡ *Twelfth Sunday after Pentecost (C)*

Here's To The Losers, Bless Them All!

LUKE 14:7-14

F rank Sinatra released a great song in 1964 called "Here's to the Losers." 1964 happens to be the year I was born, so I'm not sure what to make of that. The song is a toast to all who are unlucky in love, or alone without friends, or lost, little, least, or last in some kind of way: "Here's to the losers, bless them all."

I don't know how much of a bible reader Old Blue Eyes was, but his song is a reprisal of the beginning of Jesus' most famous sermon, the Sermon the Mount: "*Blessed are the poor in spirit, ... Blessed are those who mourn, ... Blessed are the meek, ... Blessed are those who are persecuted.*" It's like he's saying, "Here's to the losers, bless them all."

In today's Gospel reading, Jesus resumes this theme, one of his most urgent and consistent. The setting is a dinner party filled with winners, all solid citizens who are winning in life: bank presidents and managing partners and dot-com CEOs. There's also an urbane bishop and a world-traveling head of a non-profit. The text actually says that Jesus was at "the house of a leader of the Pharisees to eat a meal on the sabbath," but the anachronistic comparison is fair. Our friend Robert Capon calls the gathering a bunch of shirty Episcopalians and Presbyterians.

Our town has just undergone its annual kick-start. The University of Virginia is underway, as are most of the area schools. Virginia's head football coach Bronco Mendenhall debuts in six days. This is the time when people are figuring out how to win. Not just on the football field, but in the classroom or the boardroom or the operating room. Add to that the Gibson Room and the Donovan Room here at church—we sure hope we have a winning array of fall programs in our parish. Lots of new people move to Charlottesville this time of year to begin jobs and programs. Some of them are looking for a new church. We want to win the contest of Best Church.

The funny thing is that Jesus, the Head and Chief Cornerstone of the Church, doesn't seem very interested in winning at all, anytime, anywhere, or at anything. First, he busts the social climbers. To the shirty crowd who jockeyed themselves up to the head of the dinner party table with immediate access to both the foie gras and the Most Interesting Person To Talk To, Jesus says, "When you get invited to the party, don't make a bee-line for the top spot, but instead sit down low, next to the bathroom, out of earshot of all the inner circle kibitzing."

Well, you can imagine how this went over. Jesus dressed down the dressed-up. But then he doesn't even have the tact or manners to stop there. Next, he busts the social scorekeepers. To all the people who were congratulating themselves for a seat at the table and calculating which people had been to their party—and which people hadn't, and which people would now be issuing an invitation to their next party because they'd been seen at this party—Jesus continues his diatribe.

To all the people interested in a winning social ledger, he says, "Don't bother inviting to your party anybody who is in any position to pay the social debt back, to take you to Farmington Country Club or the C&O Restaurant. Instead, go over to Lee Park and then down to the Haven Day Shelter, where homeless people gather, and dole out your engraved invitations like a deck of cheap playing cards to anyone who can pick one up. Better yet, give them directly to the blind who can't read them and the lame who can't get there on their own, and the drunk who will guzzle down your single malt scotch like it's Schlitz Malt Liquor. In other words, 'Here's to the losers, bless them all.'"

Speaking of winning games, I have been watching episode after episode of the HBO series *Game of Thrones*. *Game of Thrones*, on one level, is all about winning. Set in a brutal fantasy world, the losers usually lose more than the game—they lose their heads or other important body parts. Yet for all of its eye-for-an-eye, head-for-a-head mentality, some of the show's most crucial and influential characters are the losers of the world, at least in terms of the power, strength, and might that the winning world so desperately values.

I'm talking about a dwarf who drinks too much, a eunuch who is, well, a eunuch, a little girl whose family has been murdered, an overweight and bookish young man who can't wield a sword but is in charge of the protection of the kingdom. The same is true in Tolkien's Middle Earth, of course, where the halfling hobbits turn out to be the ones placed at the head of the table when all is said and done.

Why is Jesus so uninterested in winning and winners? Well, if you're honest, aren't you just a little tired of playing the winning game? Does jockeying for position really satisfy you? Aren't you just a little tired of counting up who owes you what and which person you better make a good impression on if you want to get anywhere? If you are a first year at UVA, where the jockeying pressure to win is at a fever pitch, wouldn't it be good news to know that you can quit the game before it even begins?

Similarly, why is Jesus so interested in losing, losers, and the lost? Well, if you stick with that line of thinking, isn't your life filled with loss? Lost relationships, lost opportunities, lost time, and, in the end, lost lives? As grim as it is, we're all on the long trip to the boneyard. Jesus is just talking to you where you actually live, and where you will actually die. He's not really interested in the winning façade you haul around to impress people.

And it turns out that there is enormous relief in being a loser. Sam Tarly, the bookish young man in *Game of Thrones*, somehow finds the courage to kill a White Walker, the deadliest and most powerful enemy on the show. ("Even the losers get lucky sometimes," to quote a more recent song.) When asked how he managed such a monumental feat, Sam replies, "When you're nothing at all, there is no reason to be afraid."

What exactly is Jesus doing and saying at this dinner party?

One thing he is not doing is giving specific and actual instructions for your next guest list. You can follow his advice, of course, and you would have a more-than-interesting evening on your hands, which might involve broken china, stolen silver, and people passed out in the corners of your dining room. But you will have missed the deeper point.

What Jesus is doing by blessing the losers is forecasting another loss—his own on the cross. His dinner party advice about descending to the bottom rung telegraphs his descent into hell for your sake. He is the biggest loser of them all. Jesus lost his life on the cross, so that you and I would find ourselves seated at the top of the table. This is the Gospel, the free invitation to the Feast.

The point is that when you find yourself on the losing side of life, you have also found the portal to God's presence. By the way, you are there already. Jesus' stories tell us that everybody already has a seat at the table. And to the scorekeepers among the crowd, we hear that God does not count our record of wrongs against us.

That's because the Gospel is free. The Gospel is easy. The Gospel is yours already. The Gospel has nothing to do with anything you have to do. The Gospel is not about becoming a spiritual, theological, or moral winner. The Gospel does not depend on what you have done, what you are doing, or what you will do tomorrow or the next day.

Sinatra finished his beatitude ballad with a scene from another dinner party or perhaps wedding feast. He sings, "Here's the last toast of the evening: Here's to those who still believe / All the losers will be winners, all the givers shall receive." For in Jesus Christ, God has already blessed us all.

Amen.

September 18, 2016 ‡ *Fifteenth Sunday after Pentecost (C)*

Just an Unjust Steward?

LUKE 16:1-13

I n the summer of 1986, Christie and I were on an extended, low-budget backpacking trip through Europe; it was our honeymoon. We were just graduated, newly married, very young, and deeply clueless about how to navigate life as adults, much less how to be married to one another. In search of experience, I guess, we tromped from country to country, museum to museum, hostel to hostel, for five months, all with one change of skivvies.

I suppose that in the retelling, a long honeymoon through Europe sounds glamorous. It wasn't. It was filled with some high moments, yes, but also plenty of tension and homesickness. One particular moment, however, does stand out, as real today as it was 30 years ago. Disheveled, most likely in the midst of some low-simmering argument, we walked into St. Peter's Basilica in Rome, surrounded by the masses visiting the Vatican. Out of nowhere, it seemed, we found ourselves before Michelangelo's *Pietà*, almost like encountering a mountain lion around the bend of a trail.

This sculpture of the elegant but mournful Mary, holding in her lap the limp body of her crucified Son, stunned me. It felt like I was in the presence of a kind of sorrowful perfection, a nearly unbearable beauty.

The author of a *New York Times Magazine* article a few weeks ago recounts a similar moment with another masterpiece by Michelangelo. Sam Anderson and his girlfriend were also on a European trek when he encountered the massive statue of David in Florence:

> When I first saw the David in person, the only word that came to mind was "perfect." Why hadn't anyone ever told me he was perfect? I was 20 years old, exhausted, unwashed, traveling for the first time ever, ignorant of almost everything worth knowing. "Perfect," I know now, is not a terribly original response to the statue, nor a very precise one, but in that moment it filled my mind. It felt like a revolution—urgent, deep, vital, true.
>
> ...
>
> I stood there in my filthy Birkenstocks feeling a sense of religious transcendental soaring: the promise that my true self was not bound by the constraints of my childhood. ... If such perfection could exist in the world, I felt, then so many other things were suddenly possible: to live a perfect life creating perfect things, to find an ideal way to be. What was the point of anything less?

Well, however begun, it would end badly. Perfectionism in any form is a terrible curse. Oddly, in our culture, perfectionism is often emulated, striven for. It's the go-to job interview answer for "What is your greatest weakness?" "Well, you know, I'm a bit of a perfectionist ... *wink wink, nudge nudge*"—subtext: "I will perform this job without flaws." But anyone who is a perfectionist, or who lives with a perfectionist, knows the ceaseless anxiety caused by trying to find an ideal way to be. You can't be in a real relationship with someone for whom you never measure up. That includes being in a real relationship with yourself. No one ever measures up to the ideal.

Like a shot across the bow to any kind of perfection or ideal is the very odd parable that Jesus tells in today's Gospel: the Parable of the Dishonest Manager, or in other translations, the Unjust Steward. It's hard to make heads or tails of this one. Here's the cast: a rich property owner, his manager, two of the rich guy's debtors, and finally, a snitch.

Here's what happens: The snitch tells the rich guy that his manager is squandering his property. The owner brings him into his office and says, "What's this I hear? You're fired!" The manager assesses his situation and figures out a way to save his own hide. Digging and begging are out of the question, apparently the only two honest options available to him for income. The scoundrel rings up the rich man's debtors and reduces the debt, one by a half and the other by 20 percent. He figures that since he's pulled this fast one in their favor, the debtors will have to take him in when he gets kicked out of his house.

The parable's central figure then, is unjust, dishonest, and disreputable—all the traits that upstanding, God-fearing people are not supposed to be. It is certainly not an ideal way to live. But here is where the story takes a wrong turn. The property owner discovers the unjust steward's dastardly dealings and instead of throwing him in debtor's prison for further squandering his property, he applauds him! He commends dishonesty! Furthermore, Jesus holds him up as a model for "the children of light" to emulate! *What Would Jesus Do?* Commend dishonesty, apparently.

We're a long way from perfect here. The writer stunned by the *David* found himself a long way from perfect, too, the next time he visited the perfect statue 20 years later. He says, "My youthful pursuit of David-like perfection had, shall we say, not gone terribly well." His hair had thinned, his joints ached, he developed a nervous tic and social anxiety.

Anderson sagely concludes,

> Perfection, it turns out, is no way to try to live. It is a child's idea, a cartoon—this desire not to be merely good, not to do merely well, but to be faultless, to transcend everything, including the limits of yourself. It is less heroic than neurotic, and it doesn't take much analysis to get to its ugly side: a lust for control, pseudofascist purity, self-destruction. Perfection makes you flinch at yourself, flinch at the world, flinch at any contact between the two.

Accordingly, Michelangelo's *David* isn't, as it turns out, perfect.

He's got cracks in his ankles that threaten his collapse. And the real David, you probably know, was much more of a dishonest manager than an ideal king. He was an adulterer and a murderer. Oddly enough, the Lord also commended him as a man after his own heart.

King David foreshadowed another king, the one whom Pilate asked, "Are you the king of the Jews?" before he sentenced him to death. When we see this connection, we begin to see that Jesus tells this odd parable about himself. There has been no contact, presumably, between the rich landowner and the deadbeat debtors, at least nothing positive. Maybe some hounding threats to pay up or else. No positive contact, that is, until the unjust steward deals dishonestly.

At the end of the parable, however, everyone is happy. The owner may have thought he'd never see his investment, but now at least he's got 50 cents on the dollar. The debtors are now in the clear. And the dishonest manager gets a big "attaboy" and might even get his job back. If not, at least he's got a place to live without having to dig or beg.

You see who the parable's Christ figure is, don't you? The one who bridged the gap between the perfect world of the property owner and the real world of those in debt. Our reading from Timothy says it this way:

> there is one God;
>   there is also one mediator between God and humankind,
> Christ Jesus, himself human,
>   who gave himself a ransom for all ...

You may recall that He was accused of criminal activity—flouting the Law, consorting with sinners and debtors. He was crucified between two thieves. He is perfect, but there is no need to flinch at any contact with him.

You may be uncomfortable with a God who commends an unjust steward, or a Messiah who self-identifies with a dishonest manager that deals unjustly with the owner's rightful property. That may upend your version of the ideal or of justice. But I'll ask you, *Do you really want to answer to a Just Steward? Are all your debts paid in full?* I didn't think so.

The arresting power of the *Pietà* is in the way Mary grips the limp body of Jesus immediately after he has given himself as a ransom for all. Even though the sculpture is stone, the impression of lifeless flesh is overwhelming. Jesus' arm dangles off Mary's lap. His head is hanging back off the crook of Mary's arm. Oddly, he is the perfect picture of perfect peace.

Wouldn't that be something? To die to all your pursuit of perfection, the relentless struggle to measure up and instead just be held, without effort or control, in the perfect grip of the God who has thrown away all measures?

Amen.

October 10, 2010 ‡ *Eighteenth Sunday after Pentecost (C)*

Perfect Ice Cubes Once Again!

LUKE 17:11-19

Twenty-five years ago I sent Christie a card that we've kept all these years. It was back in the time when people made ice with trays in the freezer, then dumped them out into a bowl. On the front of the card, a woman stands by her freezer holding an ice tray and with breathless wonder, tears of joy in her eyes, exclaims, "Dear God, perfect ice cubes once again!" She's overcome with gratitude for the small miracle of frozen water.

In our Gospel this morning, we see a man overcome with gratitude, and for more than perfect ice cubes. In the story, 10 lepers cry out to Jesus for mercy. He tells them to go show themselves to the priests, who will, if they are healed of their leprosy, declare them clean. On the way, all 10 of the lepers find themselves healed of their leprosy.

But only one man comes back to thank Jesus. He falls before the Lord and thanks him. And Jesus says, "Get up and go your way; your faith has made you well." 10 healed, but only one made well. What is the difference between being healed and being made well?

The lepers who are healed are healed on the surface. Leprosy is a skin disease. They are externally healed. And this healing is good, obviously. It restores them to the greater community. It makes them feel better. It makes their lives better.

In this passage, I'd liken 'healing' to having the components of your life in good order: good health, good relationships, meaningful work, creative outlets, restorative leisure. I think it's what people call 'balance,' and you can read articles about finding it in every magazine ever written.

I'm first in line for this kind of healing. I like when things go well in my life. I like when "the lines are fallen unto me in pleasant places." I like when I have 'balance.' Who doesn't? But life can change in an instant, can't it?

It is that phone call that you dread. It is the growing distance between you and your husband. It is the news that your job has been eliminated, or that your best friend has a drug problem. Or maybe there is nothing obviously 'wrong' in the externals of your life, but you just can't seem to get up on Tuesday morning to put them all into balance.

It doesn't take much for me to lose my balance. As I said, I like balance. I'm all for it. I eat a healthy breakfast in hopes that the day starts off that way and keeps going in the same direction! However, the expectation that life should be balanced all the time usually ends in disappointment or anger. A more realistic way to look at life would, in the words of the old song, be, "I beg your pardon, I never promised you a rose garden."

Somehow though, I think most of us begin to expect a rose garden. We think life should go a certain way. We may even feel that we deserve for life to go well. And then we act accordingly. We do all in our power to control our lives. We exert our will to maintain balance for ourselves. And if we achieve this balance, then we have no one to thank but ourselves. We look at our healed leprosy and go show ourselves acceptable to the priests, ready to get on with our balanced lives.

The ancient Greeks called this human condition "hubris"— being out of touch with reality while overestimating one's own competence, power, and importance. The Bible calls it "the sin of pride." You and I might just call it "being selfish."

There's even an outside chance that you might actually know someone who fits this description! My wife knows a certain man who, after enjoying the amazing dinner party she prepared entirely on her own, spent the last part of that Friday evening drinking Scotch with the other men while she cleaned up! I sure don't want to meet that guy. (All my examples are obviously hypothetical anyway.)

Let's stop talking about me and start talking about *King Lear*. In that regard, I highly recommend Wendell Berry's book *Life is a Miracle: An Essay Against Modern Superstition*. By "modern superstition," Berry means the hubristic notion that life is controlled and organized by human power. He says that he reads and rereads *King Lear* to remind him of what is true about life. He points to a pivotal scene involving the Earl of Gloucester and his loyal son Edgar.

Gloucester is guilty, like King Lear, of hubris, the presumption of treating life as fully knowable, predictable, and within his control. Both his eyes are gouged out in retribution for his loyalty to King Lear. He has falsely accused and driven away Edgar. Edgar assumes the role of a madman. Gloucester wants to kill himself, so Edgar, disguised as a madman, leads his blind father to what Edgar tells him is the edge of a cliff. Gloucester, thinking that he is about to take control of his life by ending it, "falls forward and swoons."

When Gloucester returns to consciousness, he is dismayed to find himself still alive. Edgar pretends to be a passerby at the bottom of the cliff where the Earl has supposedly hurled himself. Though Gloucester says, "Away, and let me die," Edgar responds, "Thy life's a miracle. Speak yet again." In other words, how could you be alive after such a terrible fall? "Thy life's a miracle. Speak yet again." It is this line, says Berry, that "calls Gloucester back— out of hubris, ... into the properly subordinated life of human grief and joy, where change and redemption are possible."

Gloucester shows us what it means to be made well, not just to be healed. Prior to this scene, Gloucester in his anger cries, "O you mighty gods! / This world I do renounce, and, in your sights, / Shake patiently might great affliction off." I'm in charge of my life and I will do with it what I want, he says. I will find balance for myself, and if I can't, I reserve the right to take my own life. Later, after he is not healed of his physical affliction, but made well in his spirit, he prays the opposite: "You ever-gentle gods, take my breath from me. / Let not my worser spirit tempt me again / To die before you please."

To know that your own life is a miracle, a total gift, even if you are blinded like Gloucester, is to be made well. In Gloucester's case (literally) and ours (metaphorically), it is to live by faith and not by sight. To know that your life isn't even really your own possession, but that you belong to God, is to be made well. It is to live by grace and not by works.

To be made well is to know and believe what we say each Sunday as we present our offering to God: "All things come of thee, O LORD, and of thine own have we given thee." To be made well is to remember that God has given us not 50 or 75 or 99 percent of our lives, but 100 percent of all we have and all we are. Everything is sheer gift.

Ultimately, to be made well is to be delivered from hubris into humility. It is to know that you are not in control and you never will be in control and furthermore you were not meant to have control. So why not relinquish what you don't have anyway?

I have a dear friend who is going through an extremely dire medical situation. Upon his diagnosis he was forced to abandon his presumptions of control over his life. He adopted a mantra: "I can't control anything. God controls everything. And he cares for me."

After coming through a major surgery, he looked at his fingers, stretched them, moved them. He cried out, "What an incredible gift to move my fingers!" He got out of the hospital bed and took his first steps, overwhelmed with the feeling that each step is a gift from God. This friend, before his dire diagnosis, was prone to control issues. Now, though very much still living with the reality of his diagnosis, he is prone to tears of gratitude for the gift that is his life. Though still not outwardly fully healed, he has been made well. He speaks yet again, for his life is a miracle.

When you are made well, you will find that you have a whole new world of pleasure and gratitude opened up to you. It is to be able to stand at your freezer with tears of joy in your eyes and cry out, "Dear God, perfect ice cubes once again!" And you can surely, like the one leper who was not just healed but made well, come and fall at Jesus' feet and thank him.

Maybe that's why you and I are here today. Maybe we are here to be delivered from hubris into humility, where our *worser spirits* may not only be healed, but also made well. And if you're not well—and none of us is fully well—then you are definitely in the right place. Because Jesus came not for the well, but for the sick.

Amen.

November 16, 2008 ‡ *Twenty-Fourth Sunday after Pentecost (A)*

Dwarfs and Faith

MATTHEW 25:14-30

We had dinner the other night at Mas. Mas is a great restaurant with exquisite food. It is expensive, too, so a night out there is a special event. Next to our table was an attractive young couple. It looked like she had an engagement ring on, so one could hope they were celebrating young love with a delicious meal.

But, as the food came we noticed that they both got out their iPhones and started checking their email and text messaging people. They stayed on their iPhones the entire evening. They rarely talked to each other! Unless maybe they were texting each other: "Wow, this tuna is good. How is your pumpkin soup?" They were so absorbed in their virtual worlds that they missed the beauty of the real world.

That scene at Mas reminded me of a great chapter in C. S. Lewis' *The Last Battle*, the final book in his Chronicles of Narnia. It's called "How the Dwarfs Refused to Be Taken In." As the title of the book indicates, the last battle against evil is over and the characters find themselves in a verdant, heavenly, beautiful place—lush green grass, deep blue sky, a warm gentle breeze. They've reached "the country where everything is allowed," meaning that heavenly place where all your desires are right and pure and good. Everybody is in awe and wonder at the beauty of their new surroundings.

Everybody except the Dwarfs, that is. The Dwarfs won't see that they are in this beautiful place. They're obsessed with their iPhones, as it were. They think they are in a dark, cramped, smelly stable, filled with muck and dung and rotting food. The others rally around the Dwarfs and try to convince them to smell the flowers and feel the breeze and take in the beauty of the surroundings. All of this is to no avail.

Aslan, the Great Lion, comes and has compassion on the Dwarfs. He puts before them a feast of rich food and goblets of red wine. Lewis writes,

> They began eating and drinking greedily enough, but it was clear that they couldn't taste it properly. They thought they were eating and drinking only the sort of things you might find in a stable. One said he was trying to eat hay and another said he had got a bit of an old turnip. ... And they raised golden goblets of rich red wine to their lips and said "Ugh! Fancy drinking dirty water out of a trough that a donkey's been at! Never thought we'd come to this."

The scene then devolves into a fight, with every Dwarf suspecting that another Dwarf has been given better food. At the end, with bloody noses and black eyes, they all say together, "Well, at any rate there's no Humbug here. We haven't let anyone take us in. The Dwarfs are for the Dwarfs." All along the Dwarfs are wary that Aslan, the Christ-figure Lion, is a threatening menace out to do them harm. They will not let themselves believe in his goodness.

I share these scenes with you because it sets up our Gospel reading for today. It's usually called the Parable of the Talents—not "talents" as in tap dancing or acting or carpentry, but "talents" as in money. A talent was a monetary unit worth about 20 years of wages for a laborer.

What happens is a man goes away and entrusts his money to three of his servants. He gives one five talents, another two, and another one. It is interesting to note that the master doesn't leave any instructions. I guess the servants are supposed to know their master and figure out what he wants them to do with his money.

After a long time, the master returns to find that two of his servants have made more money with the sums he had entrusted to them. It's a happy reunion for those two. They must have really looked forward to his return, so they could share all that happened while he was away.

It is as if they are little children waiting for their father to return home so they can show him all the artwork they made in school that day. They know their father will come home and, no matter what the actual quality of the art is, will say, "Wow! This is amazing!" as he whispers to his wife, "What exactly is this? Is this a donkey or a space ship?" And then he grabs them up into his arms and covers their necks with kisses. The two servants aren't disappointed. The master greets them with "Well done" and "enter into the joy of your master."

Things don't turn out so well for the third servant. He has dug a hole and hidden the money underground. This may seem like a wise thing to do in today's market(!), but this servant incurs his master's wrath. There is no joy on his return for this servant, only outer darkness with weeping and gnashing of teeth.

What makes the difference in the outcome of the servants? It isn't the amount of money given to them. The five-talent and the two-talent servants are treated exactly alike. What sets the third servant apart is what he does with his one talent. He buries it. Why does he do that? The answer is in the parable. He says, "Master, I knew that you were a harsh man, reaping where you did not sow, and gathering where you did not scatter seed; so I was afraid, and I went and hid your talent in the ground."

What the servant thought of his master, that he was "a harsh man," made him bury his money in the ground. His fear of retribution paralyzed him. He flings the one talent back at the master, maybe saying something like, "Well, at any rate there's no Humbug here. I didn't lose your money. Take back what is yours." He is judged by his own words and is cast into the outer darkness.

This servant is like the Dwarfs. Just as the Dwarfs won't let themselves believe in Aslan's goodness, this servant won't let himself believe in the master's goodness. Just as the Dwarfs won't let themselves enter the joy of the beautiful scene, this servant won't

let himself enter into the joy of the master. Unlike the faithful servants, he is faithless.

Faith is what this parable is about. The two servants are commended for their faith: "Well done, good and trustworthy"—or
"faithful"—"servant." Their faith in the master's goodness allows
them to take risks with the money! It frees them up to take chances, to work hard, not worrying about the results. They know that
they will enter into the joy of their joyous master because they
know their master as a joyous man. They trust him and believe in
him, have faith in him. They are judged on their faith and happily
enter into his joy.

I find this parable so true to life. Faith and trust in God are at
the bottom of everything—that is, faith and trust in God as he has
revealed himself in Jesus Christ, as a God of grace and mercy, as
a God who has not come to condemn the world but to save it. He
is a God who loves and accepts us entirely and unconditionally
through Jesus Christ. Through faith in Christ, nothing we do can
make God love us more or love us less. Shakespeare sums up this
one-way love of God for us as he says,

> Love is not love
> Which alters when it alteration finds,
> ...
> But bears it out even to the edge of doom.

I often wonder why this message of the Gospel is rejected by some.
It is a mystery to me how such good news could be received like
an old turnip or stagnant water in a donkey's trough. It is a great
sadness to me that the news that the Bible so clearly proclaims is
either rejected full stop or turned into some bizarre version of "10
Steps to a Better Life."

But of course it happens. The faithless servant reminds us of
that this morning. No matter how often or effectively this God of
grace is preached, some people won't have it. They insist on seeing God as a bookkeeper out to settle accounts for wrong behavior.
They insist on seeing God as a Policeman out to ruin the fun. They
insist on seeing God as a condemning Judge. They insist on seeing
God as a harsh man, reaping where he does not sow. They insist on

seeing God as a God to be afraid of.

And because they won't be taken in, they are left out, like the servant, like the Dwarfs. Left out of the joy, left out in the darkness, left alone to their own devices to eek out a joyless existence where there is weeping and gnashing of teeth.

All this talk about being saved by grace through faith is humbug. They won't be taken in. It is too easy, too free, too much like a gift. But that is exactly what the Bible says it is: "For the wages of sin is death, but the free gift of God is eternal life in Christ Jesus our Lord."

What about you this morning? I long for all of us to experience God as he is—a God "whose property is always to have mercy," a God who loves you and accepts you through faith in Jesus Christ. God's love for you does not alter; it justifies you by faith alone and not by works.

Amen.

November 1, 2015 ‡ *All Saints' Day (B)*

Step Up, Jesus!

JOHN 11:32-44

Welcome to All Saints' Day, one of the most hopeful days of the year. I love this day because it sneaks in without any of the commercial trappings and anxieties of Christmas or Easter, but still packs a powerful theological punch. It is a day when the sea of troubles, ending in the annihilation of death, gives way to another reality.

As our collect says, the last word will not be sorrow, but "those ineffable joys" that God has prepared for us in heaven. When we die, we will be in God's presence, where, in the words of our reading from Revelation, "God himself will be with [us]; he will wipe every tear from [our] eyes."

The Gospel text this morning, however, begins not with God's presence, but God's absence. Mary says to Jesus, "Lord, if you had been here, my brother would not have died." Jesus is absent when Lazarus dies. Mary assumes that if Jesus had been there, this terrible thing wouldn't have happened. Mary's comment—accusation, really—is an honest starting point for people who live in a world where terrible things happen. That would be all of us. Most of us do not always feel the presence of God around us. Most of us have moments of assailing doubt and even despair.

When a terrible thing happens, like the death of someone close to us—as in the Scripture reading today, or any of the deaths that happen in life—then God can seem absent. By 'deaths,' I don't mean the end of life ('Death') but a break up, a job failure, the discovery of some painful fact about yourself or someone close to you. Where is God in all this? If he had been here, then the deaths and Death would not have happened.

The more nihilistically inclined among us tend to agree with the overall sentiment in *King Lear*, a chilling, basically hopeless play in which nearly all the principal characters die. Set 900 years before Jesus appears on the earth, it is a play in which God is conspicuously absent, and even the presence of love does not redeem anyone or anything.

Literary critic Harold Bloom, the giant in the study of Shakespeare, says, "None of us want to come away from a reading or performance of *King Lear* murmuring to ourselves that the domestic is necessarily a tragedy, but that may be the ultimate nihilism of this play." Ouch. My experience is that even the best of families have plenty of moments when Lear's message rings painfully true, and we wonder why God seems absent.

In fact, so terrible are the unfolding events in King Lear that Gloucester concludes that the gods are not just absent, but malicious: "As flies to wanton boys are we to the gods. / They kill us for their sport." In other words, the gods play around with us as cruelly as schoolboys pull wings off of flies. But your life doesn't have to be as tragic as King Lear's, nor do you have to be as despairing as Gloucester, for you to identify with Mary's accusation: *If you had been here, this wouldn't have happened. But you were not, and it did.*

The great religious mystics talk about experiencing God in his absence, otherwise known as the *via negativa*. Sounds all well and good for St. John the Divine, but, to be honest, I would much rather experience God's presence through his presence, rather than his absence.

I really can't stand the phrase "step up!" Sports commentators use it all the time: "It's time for that guy to step up," "Somebody on the defense needs to step up and make a play," and so on. They say it all the time. *Step up?* Tell me something less obvious, more original, and halfway intelligent! You know, I know, the players know, and everybody in the stands knows that somebody has got to step up.

Having said that, there are times in life when I really want to say, "Step up, Jesus! We're dying over here. It's about time for you to do something!" Mary and her sister Martha apparently feel the same way. And finally, Jesus does step up, but he's late in the game. Lazarus—his friend, their brother—has died four days earlier. If Jesus had stepped up earlier, Lazarus wouldn't have died, at least according to Mary.

Well, here's the thing: Jesus knew what he was doing. He didn't step up because it wasn't time for him to step up. In his mind and for his purpose, he stepped up at the exact right moment. When he hears that Lazarus is sick, he deliberately stays away for a few days. Why? Because Jesus has not come to the world to make good people better. Jesus has come to the world to raise dead people to life.

We like to say what Robert Capon says best:

> For Jesus came to raise the dead. He did not come to reward the rewardable, improve the improvable, or correct the correctable; he came simply to be the resurrection and the life of those who will take their stand on a death he can use instead of on a life he cannot.

Nowhere in Scripture is that clearer than in this story about Lazarus. Jesus steps up to the tomb, which is rank with four days of death, despair, decay, and doubt, and he cries in a loud voice, "Lazarus, come out!" And what must have been a moment of supreme drama, we are told, "The dead man came out," his hands, feet and face covered with cloth. Jesus simply says, "Unbind him, and let him go."

The news this All Saints' Day is not that your deaths and Death will not happen. Nor is the news that you are always guaranteed to feel God's presence. The news is way, way better than that. It is that your deaths and Death are right up God's alley, the very places he steps up and into. He goes into the tombs of your lives.

Jesus should know. He went to his own tomb. Metaphorically, his wings were torn off by the cruelty of the crucifixion. But his stone was rolled away, and he was raised. He does not simply make better; he makes new. He does not just resuscitate; he resurrects. And he will go on stepping up in this life until this life passes and death is no more, when finally "there breaks a yet more glorious day; / the King of glory passes on his way."

Amen.

November 25, 2012 ‡ *Christ the King (B)*

How Can You Stand Next to the Truth and Not See It?

JOHN 18:33-38

H*e really should have listened to his wife.* I could be talking about a number of us here, but in this case I'm talking about Pontius Pilate. According to Matthew 27:19, she sent a message to her husband not to condemn Jesus to death: "While [Pilate] was sitting on the judgment seat, his wife sent word to him, 'Have nothing to do with that innocent man, for today I have suffered a great deal because of a dream about him.'"

The weary governor tried to follow his wife's lead, reporting to the Jewish authorities that he found no guilt in the man he called "the King of the Jews." But the crowd would not have it. They demanded that Pilate deliver a death sentence. In the end, Pilate either cared too much about what the crowd thought or cared too little about the truth of Jesus' innocence. He "washed his hands and sealed his fate," as the Rolling Stones sing, ignoring his wife's message, as well as his own appraisal of the truth of the matter.

Truth is what is on Jesus' mind in this morning's Gospel. Jesus says to Pilate, "For this I was born, and for this I came into the world, to testify to the truth. Everyone who belongs to the truth listens to my voice." To this, Pilate famously responds, "What is truth?" If Jesus did answer Pilate's question, it is not recorded in

John's Gospel. Dang. I wish we had his response on record, because Pilate's question is a deep and enduring one: *What is truth?*

Children seem to know what truth is. They seem to easily grasp the concepts of right and wrong, truth and lie. Scripture says one reason for this is that "what the law requires is written on their hearts."

What is truth? Even dogs seem to know. Our dog Blue is not allowed on our bed. Yet he sneaks up there every chance he gets. When he hears my footsteps in the hallway near our bedroom, I hear the *kathunk* of Blue jumping off our bed. He then avoids eye contact with me as he slinks off to his pillow on the floor.

What is truth? Christie was at a luncheon with some of her relatives last week and her older cousin, who is prone to flourish and exaggeration, was telling a story about her daughter and granddaughters. As she held the floor, her 9-year-old granddaughter kept interrupting her: "No, Nana! That's not how it happened. That's not true, Nana. You're lying, Nana!" The granddaughter was like a little fact checker after a debate.

My parents tell me that when I was little and was accused of some family misdemeanor, I would inevitably try to talk my way out of it, proclaiming my innocence. And instead of saying, "I'm telling the truth" or "This is the truth," I would say, "I am the truth!" I left out "the way and the life," but clearly, I was struggling with messianic pretensions even at 3 years of age.

What is truth? On the most basic level of human relationship, truth is a highly prized commodity. Truth equals trust. If a teenager lies to a parent about what she has been doing or not doing, then the parent just can't trust the teenager. In most cases, the teen's freedom is compromised in the form of grounding. Not telling the truth simply violates the trust necessary in a loving relationship.

When a husband does not tell the truth to his wife, the wounds cut deep, especially when it comes to other women, money, or some activity that the husband would rather hide from the light of day. Forgiveness, by the grace of God, can happen, but trust takes a long, long time to be restored. It just does. Forgiving doesn't automatically mean forgetting. God does forgive and forget our sin, though: "I will remember their sins and their lawless deeds no more" was God's declaration in last week's reading from Hebrews. It's only God's forgiveness, God's love, that can acknowledge the truth, even when it's ugly.

"What is truth?" Pilate asks. We might be tempted to ask Pilate, "How can you stand next to the Truth and not see it?" This is literally the case, in Pilate's situation: "You have your wife's dream and your own convictions. Stick to the Truth, Pilate!"

Yet I'm thinking about the ways that all of us veer from the truth in one way or another, either by obfuscation or by downright lying. We are just too well defended when someone "speaks the truth in love." It could be an image we present to hide where we've come from or where we are going. It could be the way we highlight certain aspects of a situation but eliminate others. It could be "selective memory." A man hears what he wants to hear and disregards the rest.

Sometimes our psyches are working overtime to convince us of our innocence because we cannot face the truth of our own guilt. Jack Nicholson's courtroom rant in *A Few Good Men* was recently voted the most memorable movie quote ever. "You can't handle the truth!" he explodes to a young Tom Cruise. Sometimes we can't handle the truth of our actions, so we make up alternative stories and begin to actually believe them. And we certainly try to make everyone else believe them.

When I was 19, I crashed a car filled with my close friends. I was driving recklessly, dangerously. My best friend Drew lost his eye in the wreck. I could not accept the truth that I would do this to my friend, so I blamed the car. I told my parents and lawyers that there was a problem with the steering mechanism of the 1980 Ford Fiesta. My lawyers pursued the case with the automaker.

It wasn't until a mediation meeting with me and Drew and both of our lawyers, many months after the wreck, that I broke down and said, "It wasn't the car. It was me. The car was fine. I did it. It was my fault." My lawyers tried to convince me that it was the car's fault. I remember sitting at that conference table, looking across at Drew with his one eye and saying, "But that's not the truth. The truth is that I was driving recklessly. I crashed, and my best friend lost his eye. That is the truth." Sometimes we can't handle the truth. But as Flannery O'Connor says, "The truth does not change according to our ability to stomach it emotionally."

Have you ever spoken to someone who has nothing left to hide? He or she has been exposed in a lie, outed as a fraud. There can be a tremendous freedom in these people, as the terrible burden of projecting an image and protecting some ugly truth is taken away. A dear friend who is now serving time in prison told me that the day he was arrested was both the worst day and yet the best day of his life. I'd agree; I still remember the rush of relief as I confessed the truth of my wreck. I stopped calling it an "accident" and started calling it a "wreck."

What is truth? Jesus doesn't answer that question directly, but he does say that he has come into the world to testify to the truth. Today we use the word "testify" in court and in church, in law and in religion. To testify in court is to give a solemn attestation of the truth of a matter. To testify in church is to tell the story of what God has done. I suppose Jesus is doing a little of both here in the presence of Pilate. He is being tried in court, he is telling what God is about to do.

In that vein, a better question for Pilate might be "Who is truth?" Jesus has already answered that question, earlier in his ministry. He says, "I am the Truth." He does not have messianic pretensions—he is the Messiah. He testifies to himself as God. Pilate is standing next to the Truth.

And that is the very thing that causes his death. As the religious leaders tell Pilate a little later, when he tries to heed his wife's warning and let his prisoner go, "We have a law, and according to that law he ought to die because he has claimed to be the Son of God." Jesus spoke a truth that we could not handle, and it led him to his death.

Jesus says, "Everyone who belongs to the truth listens to my voice." Who belongs to the truth? Perhaps those who hear the truth in the prophet Isaiah, who says,

> All we like sheep have gone astray;
>   we have all turned to our own way,
> and the LORD has laid on him
>   the iniquity of us all.

What is truth? Jesus Christ is truth. And his truth is love, the love that covers the multitude of our sins.

Amen.

November 28, 2013 ‡ *Thanksgiving*

Thanksgiving and the Human Family

Virginians, being Virginians, like to claim that the first Thanksgiving took place not at Plymouth Rock, but at Berkeley Plantation in Virginia in 1619. The ships that arrived from England had a charter that required the day of arrival be observed yearly in gratitude: "*We ordaine that the day of our ships arrival at the place assigned for plantacon in the land of Virginia shall be yearly and perpetually keept holy as a day of thanksgiving to Almighty God.*" So on that first day on Virginia soil by the James River, Captain John Woodleaf held the first service of thanksgiving. We'll carry on that tradition at Christ Church later this morning!

Thanksgiving, of course, has become an annual celebration of food and family. Many families have longstanding traditions. When I was I child, my family traveled every Thanksgiving from Richmond to the Eastern Shore of Virginia, where both my parents had grown up. The undulating rhythm of the Chesapeake Bay Bridge brings back the anticipation of arrival. We rushed to get out of the house because my Aunt Mary Hamilton held a High Noon Champagne Cocktail Party for all her family and friends on the Shore. This part of the day became more interesting to me as I became an older teenager.

After the friends had departed, we gathered together for the meal. Sometimes we ate at Winona, my Uncle Herman's home overlooking Hungars Creek. Winona was built in the late 1600s, just 60 or so years after Captain Woodleaf's first Thanksgiving service. Aunts and great-aunts, uncles and great-uncles, cousins and second cousins were seated around the table (or the children's table) together. Uncle Jim always said the blessing. Neenie's pecan pie always finished the feast. And the meal was always followed by the annual backyard football game.

There was much that was wonderful about our Thanksgiving gatherings. Yet no family is immune to the difficulties that beset us all. Divorce, disease, death, and estrangement disrupt even the most hallowed traditions. My own parents divorced after I graduated from college. There are cousins I haven't seen in years. I officiated at my Uncle Jim's funeral two years ago. Such is the nature of life.

Families break apart because people are broken. Most families are no different than this priceless description of William Faulkner's family by his niece, Dean Faulkner Wells:

> Over the generations my family can claim nearly every psychological aberration: narcissism and nymphomania, alcoholism and anorexia, agoraphobia, manic depression, paranoid schizophrenia. There have been thieves, adulterers, sociopaths, killers, racists, liars, and folks suffering from panic attacks and real bad tempers, though to the best of my knowledge we've never had a barn burner or a preacher.

Sounds like my family and, I would guess, your family, although now my family does have a preacher. But Dean Faulkner Wells is just describing the human family. We're pretty much all the same. Just think about God's family as described in the Bible. Noah was a drunk, Jacob was a liar, Rahab was a prostitute, David was an adulterer and a murderer, Elijah was suicidal, and the Samaritan woman was divorced five times before shacking up with her next boyfriend!

On this "day of thanksgiving to Almighty God," no matter what permutation of friends or family we find ourselves in, what old traditions we maintain or what new ones we forge, or even if we've decided to bypass the whole affair and enjoy a quiet day alone, we might pause to give thanks that we are a human family, all connected to one another. And the comforting news is this: the God to whom we give thanks is the God who accepts us exactly as we are.

This, of course, is because of Jesus Christ who is, as we read in today's Gospel, the true bread from heaven, which gives life to the world. He died for our sins that we might be totally accepted as we are. His forgiving grace will outlast any tradition and is stronger than any divorce, disease, death, or estrangement. And even if you are alone today, or feel alone in the midst of difficulty, you are not alone. He is with you.

I'll close with a prayer from the Book of Common Prayer. It's called "A Prayer for the Human Family":

> O God, you made us in your own image and redeemed us through Jesus your Son: Look with compassion on the whole human family; take away the arrogance and hatred which infect our hearts; break down the walls that separate us; unite us in bonds of love; and work through our struggle and confusion to accomplish your purposes on earth; that, in your good time, all nations and races may serve you in harmony around your heavenly throne; through Jesus Christ our Lord.

Amen, and Happy Thanksgiving.

Bibliography

1. "Cast Away the Works of Darkness," Isaiah 2:1-5

"As G. K. Chesterton once said, ..." G. K. Chesterton, "The Maniac," *Orthodoxy* (New York: John Lane Co, 1909), 24.

"For you, little child, ..." Adapted from Église Réformée de France, Liturgie (Paris: Editions Berger Levrault, 1955), 202.

2. "Cheer Up, Sleepy Jean," Mark 13:24-37

"An article in the *New York Times* ..." Pamela Paul, "Sleep Medication: Mother's New Little Helper," *New York Times*, November 4, 2011, https://www.nytimes.com/2011/11/06/fashion/mothers-and-sleep-medication.html.

"Yes, he will come again, ..." Robert Farrar Capon, *Kingdom, Grace, Judgment* (Grand Rapids: Wm. B. Eerdmans Publishing Co, 2002), 483.

4. "Birth or Death?" Matthew 2:1-11

"For this reason, according to Eliot ..." T. S. Eliot, "Journey of the Magi," *T. S. Eliot: Collected Poems 1909-1962* (London: Faber and Faber, Ltd., 1974), 99.

"Christ says "Give me All ..." C. S. Lewis, *Mere Christianity* (New York: HarperOne, 2001), 196-97.

5. "The Voice," Matthew 3:13-17

"The boss loves your work ..." Melinda Beck, "Conquering Fear," *Wall*

Street Journal, January 2, 2011, https://www.wsj.com/articles/SB10001 4240527487041115045760598236794235988.

"As W. H. Auden says …" W. H. Auden, *For the Time Being: A Christmas Oratorio*, edited by Alan Jacobs (Princeton: Princeton UP, 2013), 64.

"As theologian Gerhard Forde says …" Gerhard Forde, *Where God Meets Man: Luther's Down-to-Earth Approach to the Gospel* (Minneapolis: Augsburg Publishing House, 1972), 14.

6. "Grace is Foolish," 1 Cor 1:10-18

"As Paul Zahl says in …" Paul Zahl, *Grace in Practice: A Theology of Everyday Life* (Grand Rapids: Wm. B. Eerdmans Publishing Co, 2007), 1.

"By now you may have …" Judith Warner, "No More Mrs. Nice Mom," *New York Times Magazine*, January 11, 2011, https://www.nytimes.com/2011/01/16/magazine/16fob-wwln-t.html.

"In contrast, Langston Hughes …" Langston Hughes, "Thank You, M'am," *Short Stories*, edited by Akiba Sullivan Harper (New York, Hill & Wang, 1996), 223-26.

7. "A Postponed Ceremony Accommodates the Naked Person," Luke 4:14-21

"The title poem of his latest book …" Christian Wiman, *Every Riven Thing* (New York: Farrar, Straus and Giroux, 2010), 24-25.

8. "All That You Can't Leave Behind," 1 Corinthians 13

"Ted Haggard has been …" "Evangelicals Sift Through Ashes of Haggard Scandal," *Religion News Service*, November 7, 2006, https://religionnews.com/2006/11/07/evangelicals-sift-through-ashes-of-haggard-scandal/.

"Well, as Fleming Rutledge says, …" Fleming Rutledge, *Help My Unbelief*, (Grand Rapids: Wm. B. Eerdmans Publishing Co, 2000), 92.

"You've got to leave it behind …" U2, "All That You Can't Leave Behind," *All That You Can't Leave Behind*, Island Records, 2000.

9. "Have You Come To Destroy Us?" Mark 1:21-28

"She wrote a remarkable …" Flannery O'Connor, *The Complete Stories* (New York: Farrar, Straus and Giroux, 1971), 488-509.

"The very first tear …" C. S. Lewis, The Voyage of the Dawn Treader (New York: HarperTrophy, 1994), 115-16.

10. "What Does the Fox Say?" Matthew 5:38-48

"A book called *Rot, Riot, and Rebellion* …" Rex Bowman and Carlos Santos, *Rot, Riot, and Rebellion* (Charlottesville: U of Virginia P, 2013).

11. "Start Acting Like a Baby!" Matthew 6:24-34

"In Washington, DC, at a Metro ..." Gene Weingarten, "Pearls Before Breakfast," *Washington Post*, April 8, 2007, https://www. washingtonpost.com/lifestyle/magazine/pearls-before-breakfast-can-one-of-the-nations-great-musicians-cut-through-the-fog-of-a-dc-rush-hour-lets-find-out/2014/09/23/8a6d46da-4331-11e4-b47c-f5889e061e5f_story.html.

12. "The End of Scorekeeping," Matthew 6:1-6

"Following the widespread acclaim ..." "Fully Validated Kanye West Retires To Quiet Farm In Iowa," *Onion*, January 6, 2011, https://www.theonion.com/fully-validated-kanye-west-retires-to-quiet-farm-in-iow-1819572025.

"In the words of a brilliant ..." "Possibly Insane Thoughts on Ash Wednesday (Written on the Occasion of a Sleepless Night)," *Mockingbird*, March 9, 2011, https://mbird.com/2011/03/possibly-insane-thoughts-on-ash/.

13. "The Crack is How the Light Gets In," Mark 1:9-15

"Leonard Cohen sings about ..." Leonard Cohen, "Anthem," *The Future*, Columbia, 1992.

"What if I forgave myself? ..." Strayed, Cheryl, *Wild* (New York: Vintage Books, 2013), 258.

"This time, in the tearing apart ..." Barbara Lundblad, "Torn Apart Forever," *Day1*, January 12, 2003, http://day1.org/535-torn_apart_forever.

14. "Considering the Great Weight," Romans 5:12-19

"He sent me an article ..." Jacqueline Davis, "LSULSU Foreign Exchange Student From Greece Gets Car Towed After Parking in 'Greeks Only' Lot," *Black Sheep Online*, February 21, 2017, https://theblacksheeponline.com/lsu/httptheblacksheeponline-comno-campuslsu-foreign-exchange-parking.

"A recent survey by the Barna ..." "New Research Explores the Changing Shape of Temptation," *Barna*, January 25, 2013, https://www.barna.com/research/new-research-explores-the-changing-shape-of-temptation/.

"Like David Byrne sings ..." Talking Heads, "Psycho Killer," *The Name of This Band Is Talking Heads*, Sire, 1982.

"Calvin: I'm getting nervous ..." Bill Watterson, "Calvin and Hobbes," December 23, 1990.

"As C. S. Lewis says, ..." C. S. Lewis, *Mere Christianity* (New York: HarperOne, 2001), 56.

15. "Where the Wild Things Are," Mark 1:9-13

"As one commentator says about ..." William L. Lane, *The Gospel of Mark* (Grand Rapids: Wm. B. Eerdmans Publishing Co, 1974), 61.

"'To most of those who have ..." William Styron, *Darkness Visible: A Memoir of Madness* (New York: Random House, 1990), 20, 76.

16. "The Devil is in the If-Thens," Luke 4:1-13

"Jeff Tweedy sings, 'When ..." Wilco, "Hell is Chrome," *A Ghost is Born*, Nonesuch, 1994.

"One begins by thinking that ..." C. S. Lewis, *God in the Dock* (Grand Rapids: Wm. B. Eerdmans Publishing Co, 2014), 124.

"Feel like I'm fallin' ..." U2, "God Part II," *Rattle and Hum*, Island Records, 1988.

17. "A Fox in the Henhouse," Luke 13:31-35

"A hen is what Jesus chooses ..." Barbara Brown Taylor, "As a Hen Gathers Her Brood," *Christian Century*, February 25, 1998, 201.

"Pelicans coach Monty Williams ..." Chris Ballard, "Ryan Anderson tries to move forward after girlfriend Gia Allemand's suicide," *Sports Illustrated*, November 10, 2014, https://www.si.com/nba/2014/11/13/ryan-anderson-gia-allemand.

19. "Semiotic Grace: The Word Beneath Our Words," Luke 15:1-3, 11b-32

"There is a *New Yorker* cartoon ..." Bruce Eric Kaplan, *New Yorker*, August 5, 1996.

"Addie Bundren, the nihilistic ..." William Faulkner, *As I Lay Dying* (New York: Vintage International, 1991), 176.

20. "Family First," Mark 3:31-35

"As Faulkner famously said ..." William Faulkner, *Requiem for a Nun* (New York: Vintage International, 2011), 69.

22. "No Defense," Matthew 27:11-54

"One said, "I have never ..." Aaron Lucchetti and Monica Langley, "Wall Street Cheers As Its Nemesis Plunges Into Crisis," *Wall Street Journal*, March 11, 2008, https://www.wsj.com/articles/SB120519411945525721.

"Commentator Cal Thomas joined ..." Cal Thomas, "Cal Thomas: Sex and the married governor," *Washington Examiner*, March 14, 2008, https://www.washingtonexaminer.com/cal-thomas-sex-and-the-married-governor.

25. "I Will Not Show You the Way," John 14:1-14

"We had been caught ..." Francis Spufford, *Unapologetic* (New York: HarperOne, 2013), 14-16.

26. "Healing Begins with the Grace of God," John 5:1-8

"Then the lion said ..." C. S. Lewis, *The Voyage of the Dawn Treader* (New York: HarperTrophy, 1994), 115-16.

27. "A Commencement for Outcasts," John 17:6-19

"Bill Watterson, of *Calvin and Hobbes* ..." "The Best Commencement Speeches, Ever," *NPR*, July 2, 2015, https://apps.npr.org/commencement/.

"Louis Armstrong's "What a ..." Louis Armstrong, "What a Wonderful World," *What a Wonderful World*, ABC, 1967.

"He responds, "But my dear ..." John Fowles, *The French Lieutenant's Woman* (Boston: Little, Brown and Co., 1969), 179.

"He finally concludes, "God ..." Georges Bernanos, *The Diary of a Country Priest*, translated by Pamela Morris (London: Boriswood, 1937), 154, 316-17.

28. "Casting Lessons," 1 Peter 5:6-11

"There is a funny *New Yorker* ..." Mort Gerberg, *New Yorker*, May 26, 2014.

""In our family," he says ..." Norman Maclean, *A River Runs Through It* (Chicago: U Chicago P, 1989), 1, 3-4, 7.

"Across the wall of the world ..." Maya Angelou, "On the Pulse of Morning," *The Complete Collected Poems of Maya Angelou* (New York: Random House, 2015), 263.

29. "I Can't Get No Satisfaction," John 14:8-17, 25-27

"But Mick Jagger was right ..." Rolling Stones, "Satisfaction," *Out of Our Heads*, Decca, 1965.

"Sarah Jane Bradley was an ..." Nellie Bowles, "These Millennials Got New Roommates. They're Nuns," *New York Times*, May 31, 2019, https://www.nytimes.com/2019/05/31/style/milliennial-nuns-spiritual-quest.html.

30. "The Gospel According to Quasimodo," Romans 5:1-5

"As it turns out, that's ..." Ozgun Atasoy, "You Are Less Beautiful Than You Think," *Scientific American*, May 21, 2013, https://www.scientificamerican.com/article/you-are-less-beautiful-than-you-think/.

31. "By Faith and Not By Sight," Genesis 6:9-22, 7:24, 8:14-19

"Hemingway said, "The world breaks ..." Ernest Hemingway, *A Farewell to Arms* (New York: Scribner, 2012), 318.

32. "Bear One Another's Burdens," Galatians 6:1-16

"On Dec. 14, 1934, a failed ..." David Brooks, "Bill Wilson's Gospel," *New York Times*, June 28, 2010, https://www.nytimes.com/2010/06/29/opinion/29brooks.html.

""Help," he said, "is giving ..." Norman Maclean, *A River Runs Through It* (Chicago: U Chicago P, 1989), 81.

33. "I Do Not Do What I Want To Do," Romans 7:15-25

"As author Ian McEwan says, ..." Ian McEwan, *Solar* (New York: Anchor, 2011), 217.

34. "Hell in the Parking Lot," Colossians 1:1-14

"The session described in the ..." Richard Powers, *The Overstory* (New York: W. W. Norton, 2018), 400, 403.

35. "What You Need Is What Will Last," Luke 10:38-42

"The Stones sang, "You can't ..." Rolling Stones, "You Can't Always Get What You Want," *Let it Bleed*, Decca, 1969.

36. "Jesus Comes Aboard the Ship of Fools," Matthew 14:22-33

"In one as in the other ..." Frederick Buechner, *Beyond Words* (New York: HarperCollins, 2004), 277.

"As Dylan sings, "Try imagining ..." Bob Dylan, "Shelter from the Storm," *Blood on the Tracks*, Columbia, 1975.

39. "Here's to the Losers, Bless them All!" Luke 14:7-14

"He sings, "Here's to the ..." Frank Sinatra, "Here's to the Losers," *Softly, As I Leave You,* Reprise, 1964.

40. "Just an Unjust Steward," Luke 16:1-13

"When I first saw the David ..." Sam Anderson, "David's Ankles: How Imperfections Could Bring Down the World's Most Perfect Statue," *New York Times*, August 17, 2016, https://www.nytimes.com/2016/08/21/magazine/davids-ankles-how-imperfections-could-bring-down-the-worlds-most-perfect-statue.html.

41. "Perfect Ice Cubs Once Again," Luke 17:11-19

"It is this line, says Berry ..." Wendell Berry, *Life is a Miracle* (Berkeley: Counterpoint, 2000), 5.

42. "Dwarfs and Faith," Matthew 25:14-30

"They've reached "the country where ..." C. S. Lewis, *The Last Battle* (New York: HarperCollins, 1994), 172, 184-85.

43. "Step Up, Jesus!" John 11:32-44

"Literary critic Harold Bloom, the ..." Harold Bloom, "Shakespeare and the Value of Love," Tanner Lectures on Human Values, Princeton University, 1995, 196-97.

"For Jesus came to raise ..." Robert Farrar Capon, *Kingdom, Grace, Judgment* (Grand Rapids: Wm. B. Eerdmans Publishing Co, 2002), 317.

44. "How Can You Stand Next to the Truth and Not See It?" John 18:33-38

"But as Flannery O'Connor says ..." Flannery O'Connor, *The Habit of Being* (New York: Farrar, Straus and Giroux, 1999), 100.

45. "Thanksgiving and the Human Family"

"Over the generations my family ..." Dean Faulkner Wells, *Every Day by the Sun: A Memoir of the Faulkners of Mississippi* (New York: Broadway, 2011), 2-3.

ACKNOWLEDGMENTS

For making this collection of sermons possible,
I wish to thank the Mockingbird staff. Special
thanks to Dave Zahl for the idea and prodding, as
well as to Henry Harris, Kendall Gunter, Margaret
Pope, and CJ Green for seeing the project through
to completion. I'd also like to thank the fellow
preachers of the Gospel who have shared the
Christ Church pulpit with me during my tenure as
rector: Dave Johnson, Justin Holcomb, Dave Zahl,
Willis Logan, Marilu Thomas, and Josh Bascom.
It has been an honor to serve alongside of each of
these excellent ministers.

ABOUT THE AUTHOR

Paul Walker is the 12th Rector of Christ
Episcopal Church (Charlottesville, Virginia).
He was born and raised in Richmond, Virginia,
and attended the University of Virginia and
Virginia Theological Seminary. Previously, he
served at the Cathedral Church of the Advent
(Birmingham, Alabama) from 2001 to 2004.
Paul is married to Christie and they have three
children, Hilary, Glen, and Rob.

ABOUT MOCKINGBIRD

Founded in 2007, Mockingbird is an organization devoted to connecting the Christian faith with the realities of everyday life in fresh and down-to-earth ways. We do this primarily, but not exclusively, through our publications, conferences, and online resources. To find out more, visit us at mbird. com or e-mail us at info@mbird.com.

CPSIA information can be obtained
at www.ICGtesting.com
Printed in the USA
FSHW010116010420
68685FS